DEPARTMENT OF TRANSPORT

THE MERCHANT SHIPPING ACT 1894

mv **HERALD OF FREE ENTERPRISE**

Report of Court No. 8074.

Formal Investigation

London
Her Majesty's Stationery Office

© Crown copyright 1987
   First published 1987
   Third Impression 1988

MV HERALD OF FREE ENTERPRISE

REPORT OF COURT NO. 8074 FORMAL INVESTIGATION

ISBN 0 11 550828 7

ADDENDUM BY MR JUSTICE SHEEN

Paragraph 19.6

In this paragraph it is stated that certain handwritten comments on a memorandum dated 10 February 1983 were written by Mr Michael Ayers, who did not give evidence at the investigation. Mr Michael Ayers has drawn my attention to the fact that he did not write any of the comments to which specific reference is made. No criticism of Mr Michael Ayers was made or intended. The sentence on page 28 should be read as if the words "Mr Michael Ayers" had been deleted.

Department of Transport
September 1987

London: Her Majesty's Stationery Office

ISBN 0 11 550828 7

THE MERCHANT SHIPPING ACT, 1970

The Roll on/Roll off passenger and freight ferry

HERALD OF FREE ENTERPRISE

registered at the port of Dover (O.N.379260)

Order as to costs

By virtue of the jurisdiction conferred on me by subsection (5) of section 56 of the Merchant Shipping Act 1970 I make the following orders with regard to the costs of the investigation:

(1)   That the Secretary of State for transport pay the sum of £39,675 to Messrs Keeble Crewson and Bridge of 8 Abbey Walk, Grimsby, to cover the costs of legal representation for Mr. Mark Victor Stanley.

(2)   That the Secretary of State for Transport pay the sum of £10,000 to Messrs Ince and Company of Knollys House, 11 Byward Street, London E.C.3., as a contribution towards the costs of legal representation for surviving passengers and next-of-kin of the deceased.

(3)   That Townsend Car Ferries Limited pay the sum of £50,000 to Messrs Steggles Palmer of 2 Bedford Row, W.C.1., the solicitors for the National Union of Seamen and certain surviving crew members and dependants of those members of the crew who lost their lives.

(4)   That the Secretary of State for Transport pay the sum of £25,000 to Messrs Ingledew, Brown, Bennison and Garrett of 26 Creechurch Lane, E.C.3., towards the costs of legal representation for Captain David Lewry and Mr. Leslie Sabel.

(5)   That Townsend Car Ferries Limited pay the sum of £350,000 to the Secretary of State for Transport towards the costs of the Investigation.

Dated this 29th day of July 1987   Wreck Commissioner

Hon. Mr. Justice Sheen, Wreck Commissioner

THE MERCHANT SHIPPING ACT 1970

DECISION OF THE COURT

The Roll on/Roll off passenger and freight ferry

HERALD OF FREE ENTERPRISE

registered at the port of Dover (O.N.379260)

In the matter of a Formal Investigation held at Church House, Westminster and at Alexandra House, Kingsway, W.C.1. on 29 days between the 27th day of April 1987 and the 12th day of June 1987 before the Honourable Mr. Justice Sheen, assisted by E. C. B. Corlett, O.B.E., M.A., Ph.D., F.Eng., F.R.I.N.A., Mr. C. A. Sinclair, C.Eng., F.R.I.N.A., F.I.Mar.E., F.C.M.S., Commodore G. G. Greenfield, R.D., R.N.R., F.N.I., and Captain E. G. Venables into the circumstances attending the capsizing of the Roll on/Roll off passenger ferry *HERALD OF FREE ENTERPRISE* in the approaches to the port of Zeebrugge with the loss of 188 lives on the 6th day of March 1987.

The Court, having carefully inquired into the circumstances attending the above-mentioned shipping casualty, finds, for the reasons stated in the Report, that the capsizing of the *HERALD OF FREE ENTERPRISE* was partly caused or contributed to by serious negligence in the discharge of their duties by Captain David Lewry (Master), Mr. Leslie Sabel (Chief Officer) and Mr. Mark Victor Stanley (Assistant bosun), and partly caused or contributed to by the fault of Townsend Car Ferries Limited (the Owners). The court suspends the certificate of the said Captain David Lewry for a period of one year from the 24th July 1987. The Court suspends the certificate of the said Mr. Leslie Sabel for a period of two years from the 24th July 1987.

Dated this 24th day of July 1987.

Hon. Mr. Justice Sheen, Wreck Commissioner

We concur in the above decision.

Dr. E. Corlett, Assessor
Mr. C. A. Sinclair, Assessor
Commodore G. G. Greenfield, Assessor
Captain E. G. Venables, Assessor

Index to Report

PART I

PART II

THE HERALD OF FREE ENTERPRISE

PART 1

1. *Introduction*

1.1   On the 6th March 1987 the Roll on/Roll off passenger and freight ferry *HERALD OF FREE ENTERPRISE* under the command of Captain David Lewry sailed from Number 12 berth in the inner harbour at Zeebrugge at 18.05 G.M.T. The *HERALD* was manned by a crew of 80 hands all told and was laden with 81 cars, 47 freight vehicles and three other vehicles.

1.2   Approximately 459 passengers had embarked for the voyage to Dover, which they expected to be completed without incident in the prevailing good weather. There was a light easterly breeze and very little sea or swell. The *HERALD* passed the outer mole at 18.24. She capsized about four minutes later. During the final moments the *HERALD* turned rapidly to starboard and was prevented from sinking totally by reason only that her port side took the ground in shallow water. The *HERALD* came to rest on a heading of 136° with her starboard side above the surface. Water rapidly filled the ship below the surface level with the result that not less than 150 passengers and 38 members of the crew lost their lives. Many others were injured. The position in which the *HERALD* came to rest was less than 7 cables from the harbour entrance and was latitude 51° 22′ 28.5″ North, longitude 3° 11′ 26″ East.

2. *Order for Formal Investigation*

2.1   Three days later the Secretary of State for Transport (hereinafter "the Secretary of State") in exercise of the powers vested in him by Section 55 of the Merchant Shipping Act 1970 ordered a Formal Investigation to be held by a Wreck Commissioner into the circumstances giving rise to this casualty. The Treasury Solicitor instructed Mr. David Steel Q.C. and Mr. John Reeder to represent the Secretary of State and to have conduct of the Investigation.

2.2   It is appropriate to record at the outset that due to the exertions of all the lawyers involved, in particular, to the industry of the Treasury Solicitor's Department and of Messrs. Norton, Rose, Botterell and Roche and all their respective Counsel the Investigation was opened on Monday 27 April 1987, only 7 weeks after the catastrophe. That was a remarkable achievement. Statements had to be taken from very many witnesses and a large number of documents had to be disclosed, read, copied, marshalled and digested. Nevertheless, the commencement of an Investigation within a few weeks should not be regarded as exceptional. There are good reasons why it is desirable that the decision whether or not to hold a Formal Investigation should be made without delay. It is in the interest of all parties and of many others who may be affected by a casualty that if an Investigation is to be held, it should commence at the earliest possible moment.

2.3   The reasons for this may be self-evident, but we draw attention to the following. (1) It is desirable that eye-witnesses should give their evidence before their memories fade or play them false, even though for some time after a catastrophe witnesses may be affected by injury, shock and emotion. The Court will always make allowance for these factors. (2) If an Investigation into the causes of a casualty has the result that lessons are learned, which may make for greater safety in the future, then the sooner those lessons are learned the better for the whole community. (3) It is inevitable that a casualty, such as the one under investigation, will give rise to much rumour and speculation as to who was responsible. Such rumours and speculation should be ended. Those at whom the finger of blame may be pointed are entitled to be heard without delay. (4) Those who have been bereaved will wish to know as soon as possible the reason for their bereavement in the hope that thereafter time will begin to heal the wounds caused by their grievous losses.

3. The Parties

3.1   At the time of the casualty the *HERALD* was owned by Townsend Car Ferries Limited (hereinafter "the Company"), which was a subsidiary of the Peninsular and Oriental Steam Navigation Company (hereinafter "P. & O."). Notice of the Investigation dated 13 March 1987 was served upon the Company. Mr. Anthony Clarke Q.C., Mr. Nigel Teare and Mr. Jeremy Russell were instructed by Messrs. Norton, Rose, Botterell and Roche to appear on behalf of the Company.

3.2   By a peculiar constitutional anomaly, which is given statutory recognition in the Merchant Shipping (Formal Investigations) Rules 1985, a distinction is drawn between the Secretary of State and his Department. This topic is referred to again in paragraph 60 of this Report. The Department of Transport (hereinafter "the Department"), which is responsible for regulations concerning the safety of life at sea, was represented by Mr. Richard Stone Q.C., and Miss V. Selveratnam, who were also instructed by the Treasury Solicitor.

3.3   Other parties who took part in the Investigation were represented as follows. Miss Belinda Bucknall, instructed by Messrs. Ingledew, Brown, Bennison and Garrett, appeared on behalf of the Master, Captain David Lewry, and the Chief Officer, Mr. Leslie Sabel. Mr. T. Brenton, instructed by Messrs. Sinclair, Roche and Temperley, appeared on behalf of Captain Kirby, who was the Senior Master of the *HERALD*. Mr R. Owen and Mr. M. Ford, instructed by Messrs, Steggles Palmer, appeared on behalf of the National Union of Seamen and certain surviving crew members and also on behalf of next-of-kin and other dependants of those members of the crew who lost their lives. Mr. S. Miller, instructed by Messrs. Keeble, Crewson and Bridge, appeared on behalf of Mr. Victory Stanley, who was the assistant bosun. Mr. C. Haddon-Cave, instructed by a group of Solicitors, appeared on behalf of the next-of-kin and dependants of those passengers who lost their lives and also on behalf of certain passengers who were injured.

4. Description of the HERALD

4.1   The *HERALD* was a triple screw Ro/Ro passenger/vehicle ferry built by Schichau Unterweser AG, Bremerhaven in 1980. She was registered at Dover, official number 379260 and was 7951.44 tonnes gross and 3439.05 tonnes net register. Her length was 131.9 m overall, 121.1 m between perpendiculars, breadth 22.7 m moulded. Propulsion was provided by three Sulzer 12ZV 40/48 internal combustion engines, each developing 9,000 BHP at the maximum continuous rating and 8,000 BHP at the continuous service rating. Each engine drove a controllable pitch propeller via a 2.36:1 ratio reduction gear box. Electrical power was provided by three internal combustion driven alternators, each of 1063 kVA capacity. Shaft driven alternators provided power for bow thrusters and a feathering bow propeller used in the docking mode. Emergency power was provided by a diesel driven alternator of 515 kVA capacity. Engine control arrangements were generally to unmanned machinery space requirements although the machinery control room and spaces were constantly manned. The controllable pitch propellers could be controlled from the wheelhouse or the machinery control room. The vessel was capable of a service speed of 22 knots. Comprehensive navigational and communications equipment was fitted.

4.2   The *HERALD* was class +100A2 "Ferry" with Lloyd's Register of Shipping and had a Loadline Certificate valid until 25 March 1990.

4.3   The ship was of all welded steel construction, with a raked stem and transom stern. A double bottom extended from frame 25 to frame 149. Above the level of the tank tops there were 8 decks, the uppermost being A deck and the lowest H deck, which was below the main or (bulkhead) deck. H deck was sub-divided by 13 watertight bulkheads and had 9 watertight doors for access between compartments. There were 4 watertight flats devoted to passenger accommodation and store spaces. Compartments between the watertight bulkheads were devoted to steering gears (bow and stern) main and auxiliary machinery, fuel and fresh water storage, sewage plant, ballast tanks and voids.

4.4   The main deck (G deck) was enclosed by a full superstructure and was a through vehicle deck with a single weathertight door at stern, with a clear opening of 8.5 m × 4.73 m, and double weathertight doors at bow with a clear opening of 6.0 m × 4.9 m. At each side there was a mezzanine deck (F deck). The emergency generator was situated on the starboard side of F deck. The remaining space both port and starboard sides was crew accommodation.

4.5   E deck was a second vehicle deck. It was a through deck enclosed by sidehouses between frames 21 and 159 port and starboard, open at the after end and closed forward by a weathertight door, with a clear opening 6 m × 4.9 m. There was a suspended vehicle platform deck (D deck) on port and starboard sides within this vehicle space.

4.6   C deck extended to the full breadth of ship and housed passenger areas and the galley. B deck housed passenger areas and a galley; mess rooms (P.O and Officers) on the port side and ratings mess room and accommodation on the starboard side. Officers' accommodation and the radio room were situated on A deck. The wheel house was situated at a half deck level between A and B decks.

4.7   Access between decks A to G was by way of staircases at port and starboard sides at aft end, midships and fore end. The staircases at the fore end continued down to H deck. (We comment on this feature of the design in Part II of this Report.)

4.8   The vessel was built to comply with the Merchant Shipping (Passenger Ship Construction) Rules 1980 and SOLAS 1974. Although the keel was laid in February 1979 and the ship was initially regarded as a new ship under the 1965 Rules, it was updated to comply with later Rules and Regulations and carried all the appropriate lifesaving appliances. At 6 March 1987 the ship was in possession of a Class II Passenger Certificate. This Passenger Ship Safety Certificate for a short international voyage (not more than 600 miles from first to final port) was issued as a temporary extension from 11 February 1987 for a period of one month. (The *HERALD* was about to undergo her annual refit). It showed that in the C1 condition, that is to say with a freeboard of 1110 mm, the ship was entitled to carry a total of 630 persons including crew. In the C2 condition the ship was required to have a freeboard of 1310mm. In this condition she was permitted to carry a total of 1400 persons. In the C2 condition the draught of the ship was not permitted to exceed 5.5 m moulded. If carrying not more than 630 persons her draught could exceed 5.5 m but it was not permitted to exceed 5.7 m moulded. Accordingly it was essential that the number of passengers and the draught of the ship should be known before the commencement of each voyage.

5. *Bow and stern doors*

It is necessary to give a more detailed description of the lower car deck (G deck) and its doors.

5.1   The *HERALD*, in common with other modern Ro/Ro ferries, had an enclosed superstructure above the bulkhead deck. For this to be considered as contributing to the ship's intact stability it must be weathertight. Scuppers were provided on the bulkhead deck capable of draining off any minor quantity of water which may accumulate through weather, fire fighting, washing decks or pipe leakages. These scuppers were capable of handling about 3/400 tons per hour, using some 20 seven-inch drain pipes with non-return valves on each side of the ship.

5.2   It should be noted that the term "weathertight" does not imply that the condition is of a lower order of tightness than "watertight". Watertight is applied to doors and bulkheads where there is the possibility of water accumulating at either side. Weathertight applies to doors or openings which are only required to prevent the ingress of water from the side exposed to the weather. When testing for weathertightness, the procedure is to hose test from the weather side only, whereas when testing for watertightness the hose test would be applied from both sides. At the bow there were inner and outer doors. At the stern only outer doors were fitted. The bow and stern doors were required to be weathertight.

5.3   All the vehicle deck bow and stern doors were hydraulically operated and were so arranged that they swung horizontally about vertical axes, on radius arms. Their weight and movement were supported by rubberised rollers (or wheels). In order to support the bow and stern doors whilst being opened or closed, the vessel's belting at both the bow and the stern was extended in the form of a horizontal platform which was shaped to fit the fenders of the ramps, thereby allowing the vessel to be held tight in the berth when loading and discharging. The doors stowed against the ship's sides when open. They met at the centre line so that one door stowed to port and the other to starboard. The inner bow doors were lock gate type. They opened in a forward direction and stowed against longitudinal bulkheads to port and starboard. The construction of the doors was such that they were able to withstand the normal forces anticipated in the bow and stern areas of the vessel. Structurally they were required to be at least as strong as a fully plated bow and stern. They also had sufficient rigidity to prevent distortion during the opening and closing operations. Although the spade at the level of the belting deflected the seas at the bow when the vessel was proceeding at full speed, in calculating the strength of the bow doors there was no reduction in scantlings because of this factor.

5.4   In the closed position, watertightness was maintained by compressing tubular neoprene seals around the outer periphery of the doors. Closure of the doors and the compression on these seals was maintained by a system of clamps and dogs which were hydraulically operated. The dogs were forced by hydraulic cylinders into box shaped blind-ended apertures in the deck head and on the car deck. There were limit switches which controlled the distance during which full pressure needed to be applied.

5.5   The hydraulic pressure to the opening/closing rams was piped through directional control valves which were actuated by a lever in the control box. This control lever, like the clamping lever, returned to the off position when the operator released it. There was an alarm bell which rang whilst the doors were in motion. The bell was a safety device to prevent anyone being caught unawares, and should not have been switched off.

5.6   There is no reason to think that there was any fault which would have prevented the doors from being closed hydraulically. There was some evidence from a Mr. John Calderwood, who was a freight driver, that he returned to G deck before the ship sailed and that he heard a loud metallic bang which made him think that the crew were having difficulty in closing the bow doors. The Court were not convinced that Mr. Calderwood had an accurate recollection of the events which he endeavoured to describe.

6. *Life-saving apparatus*

The *HERALD* carried the following life-saving apparatus:

8 Lifeboats (4 motor)	for 630 persons
16 Inflatable liferafts associated with M.E.S.	for 672 persons
7 Throwover liferafts	for 175 persons
5 Buoyant apparatus	for 70 persons
20 Lifebuoys	
1525 Lifejackets (including 139 for persons weighing less than 32 kg)	

Embarkation to the lifeboats was at E deck level. The *HERALD* was equipped with a Marine Escape System (M.E.S.) on each side of D deck.
The *HERALD* not only conformed with, but carried equipment in excess of, statutory requirements.

7. *Manning*

7.1   The *HERALD* and her two sister-ships were built for the Dover-Calais run. They were built with very powerful engines, capable of rapid acceleration, in order to make the crossing at high speed. It was intended that they would disembark their passengers and vehicles rapidly and then without any delay embark passengers and vehicles for the return voyage. On the Dover-Calais run these ships are manned by a complement of a Master, two Chief Officers and a Second Officer. The officers are required to work 12 hours on and not less than 24 hours off. In contrast, each crew was on board for 24 hours and then had 48 hours ashore.

7.2 The sea passage between Dover and Zeebrugge takes 4½ hours, which is substantially longer than the passage between Dover and Calais and which, therefore, gives the officers more time to relax. For this reason the Company employed a Master and two deck officers on this run. They were entitled to do so. The Court can see no reason why the *HERALD* could not have been safely and efficiently operated on the Dover-Zeebrugge run with this number of officers, if proper thought had been given to the organisation of their duties. We return to consider that organisation later, but it is now necessary to describe in some detail the port facilities at Zeebrugge and their consequences.

7.3 *Zeebrugge*

No. 12 berth at Zeebrugge was a single level berth, not capable of loading both E and G decks simultaneously, as at the berths in Dover and Calais for which the ship was designed. The ramp at Zeebrugge was designed for loading on to the bulkhead deck of single deck ferries. In order to load the upper deck of the *HERALD* it was necessary to raise the ramp so that it led upwards to E deck. When loading or unloading at high water spring tides the ramp could not be elevated sufficiently to reach E deck. As the ships berthed bows to this berth it was necessary to trim the ship by the head to allow the raised ramp to reach E deck. To achieve this trim ballast tanks Nos. 14 and 3 were filled. No. 14 was a deep tank and had a capacity of 268 cu.m No. 3 was a port double bottom tank with a capacity of 42 cu.m. The general practice was to start flooding No. 14 deep tank about two hours before arrival in order to berth with the requisite trim by the head. The forward tanks were on the main ballast line but were not connected to high capacity pumps as were the heeling tanks which were used for keeping the ship upright during loading. The ballast system could fill or empty No. 14 ballast tank at a rate of 115–120 tonnes per hour.

7.4 Thus at Zeebrugge the turn-round was different from the turn-round at Calais in four main respects. At Zeebrugge (1) only two deck officers were available, (2) only one deck could be loaded at a time, (3) it was frequently necessary to trim the ship by the head, and (4) the bow doors could be closed at the berth. Because of these differences, with proper thought the duties of the deck officers at Zeebrugge would have been organized differently from their duties at Calais. No such thought was given to the matter, with the result that immediately loading was complete the Chief Officer felt under pressure to leave G deck to go to his harbour station on the bridge. This is amplified later in this Report.

7.5 Three crews and five sets of officers were employed in manning the *HERALD*. Accordingly the officers did not always have the same crew. This made it not merely desirable but essential that there should be uniformity in the duties of each set of officers and of the members of each crew. A competent superintendent, applying his mind to the organisation of the officers and crew, would have issued "Company Standing Orders", which would have been uniform for all the ships of one class. They would have covered all aspects of organisation, not only for the Calais run but also for the Zeebrugge run when the ship carried only two deck officers in addition to the Master. This had not been done. The Company had issued Standing Orders to the *HERALD* entitled "Ship's Standing Orders", which were in force in March 1987 and which display a lack of proper thought. We will revert to those orders later. Since the casualty the Company has given thought to this topic and has issued new standing orders.

8. *The condition of the HERALD on departure*

8.1 On the night of the casualty the *HERALD* was trimmed by the head in order to load E deck. That deck was completed before G deck, and stripping of No. 14 deep tank commenced at about 17.40 G.M.T. No. 3 tank was to follow thereafter. The Department has estimated that by departure some 50 tonnes had been pumped from No. 14 tank and by the time of the capsize a total of some 100 tonnes had been stripped out.

5

8.2 The *HERALD* was to make the voyage in the C1 condition. In that condition the ship was of one compartment standard, in other words capable of accepting damage to any one compartment in the ship without either losing stability or submerging the margin line at any time during flooding. (The margin line is an imaginary line 76 mm below the bulkhead deck.) The ship's displacement on sailing consisted of her lightship together with the sum of all consumables on board (fuel oil, diesel oil, fresh water and stores etc.) the weight of her crew and their effects and the weight of the passengers, cars, luggage, commercial vehicles and coaches.

8.3 The condition of the *HERALD* upon her departure was calculated by the Department as follows:-

Displacement	—	8874 tonnes
Mean draught		
(USK)	—	5.68 m
Trim	—	0.75 m (by head)
Draught forward	—	6.06 m
Draught aft	—	5.31 m
Vertical centre of		
gravity (fluid)	—	9.73 m
GMf	—	2.09 m

8.4 When the full-scale experiment using the *PRIDE OF FREE ENTERPRISE* was undertaken in early June at Zeebrugge it was found that the ship could not accommodate the weight of vehicles calculated from the Builder's lightship and from the declared weights. To investigate the reason for this, 105 vehicles incoming to the United Kingdom were weighed at Dover. It was found that there was a general excess of actual as compared with waybill weights. The average excess was approximately 13% per vehicle. There was another reason also. Detailed checks upon the lightship weight of the *PRIDE* and the *SPIRIT* indicated that both ships were heavier than the Builder's lightship by about 270 tonnes. Investigation of the history of each vessel showed that modifications had increased the weight of both vessels by about 115 tonnes. The balance of the weight increase known to be present in the *PRIDE* and *SPIRIT* (about 148 tonnes) must be attributed to the accumulation of dunnage, stores, paint and other growth items. Modifications to the *HERALD* are known to be 102 tonnes. From this it follows that the *HERALD* lightship was probably increased by about 250–270 tonnes above the Builder's lightship.

8.5 The Department computed alternative departure and casualty conditions using an increased lightship and also an additional weight per vehicle as disclosed by the test weighings. For the purpose of this computation the additional weight for the vehicles was assumed conservatively to be only 10%. These calculations form an upper limit for the night of the casualty, while calculations made from the builder's lightship and waybill weights form a lower limit. The departure condition of the *HERALD* as calculated on the basis of the upper limit was:

Displacement	—	9250 tonnes
Mean draught		
(USK)	—	5.85 m
Trim	—	0.83 m
Draught forward	—	6.26 m
Draught aft	—	5.43 m
Vertical centre of		
gravity (fluid)	—	9.75 m
GMf	—	2.04 m

It will be seen that this condition would be overloaded by some 0.13 m. The Court is satisfied that at departure the *HERALD* had a mean draught of between 5.68 m and 5.85 m with a trim by the head of about 0.8 m. The probability is that the draught and trim approached the upper limit condition and that the ship was in fact overloaded significantly at departure. This overload, however, was not in any way causative of the casualty. Its real significance is in the lessons to be learned from it. It demonstrates the need for more information about the weight of cargo to be loaded and the desirability of fitting draught indicators.

9. *The manoeuvres leading to the capsize*

9.1   Upon departure the *HERALD* went astern from the berth, turned to starboard at the end of the Kennedy Quay and proceeded to sea through the inner harbour. The *HERALD* was being manoeuvred on combinators. A combinator is an engine control on the bridge. At any one position the propeller pitch is combined with revolutions and engine throttle to give the desired speed. The wing engines and propellers were not controlled by a true combinator as the machinery ran at constant revolutions. The control only affected pitch and the engine took up the required load automatically. The centre engine was controlled by a true combinator with a pitch control trimming wheel which was set at the maximum value. The engine settings had been adjusted, however, so as not to overload it.

9.2   The Master and deck officers testified that when entering or leaving Zeebrugge with the ship trimmed by the head care was taken to restrict the speed to a level which would avoid water coming over the bow spade. The Second Officer said that he would watch the spade and if water came on top of it he would inform the Master, who would slacken speed. The Master and the Chief Officer gave speeds for Combinator 4 and Combinator 6 settings which appear to be significantly below those of which the ship was actually capable.

Thus Captain Lewry stated that at Combinator 4 the speed would be 10–12 knots while at 6 it would reach 15–16 knots. The corresponding figures given by Mr. Sabel were 7 knots and 12 knots or a little higher. The *PRIDE* experiment showed the vessel would have been capable of a speed of approximately 14 knots on Combinator 4 setting and $17\frac{1}{2}$–18 knots on Combinator 6.

9.3   The *SPIRIT* Class were designed for rapid acceleration with engines capable of going from idle to full load rapidly and with propellers designed to accept this increasing load without difficulty. On passing the Outer Mole Captain Lewry set Combinator 6 on all three engines. The *HERALD* accelerated rapidly from 14 knots to a possible ultimate speed of 18 knots. Towards the end of this acceleration the combination of dynamic sinkage, or squat, and an increase in bow wave height caused water to enter over the spade and flow aft into G deck. The fact that Captain Lewry set Combinator 6 is strange in the light of the evidence given by himself and by the two Mates that they restricted the Combinator settings, until the bow tank had been pumped out fully, to levels at which water did not come over the spade. Both the model tests and the *Pride* experiment indicated clearly that at Combinator 6 the bow wave would be well up the bow doors, i.e. perhaps 2 m above the level of the top of the spade. The Court has concluded that on the evening of the 6th March Captain Lewry did not follow the practice, which he described, of restricting speed so that water did not come above the spade. The Court is satisfied that the rate of inflow of water was large and increased progressively as the ship dug the bow spade deeper into the water and decreased the freeboard forward. A large quantity of water entered G deck and caused an initial lurch to port due to free surface instability which was extremely rapid and reached perhaps 30°. The water collected in the port wing of the vehicle deck and the ship became stable again at a large angle of loll. Water in large quantities continued to flood through the open bow doors aperture. Thereafter the *HERALD* capsized to port rather more slowly until eventually she was at more than 90°. It is not possible to say whether the ship reached more than 90° while still floating or whether this was only when she reached the sea bed. There is some reason for thinking that the ship floated more or less on her beam ends for about a minute before finally resting on the sea bed.

9.4   The events from leaving the end of the berth jetty up to the final capsize were investigated by British Maritime Technology. Experimental work was also carried out by a full-scale trial of the *PRIDE* at Zeebrugge. An account of this experimental work is set out in Appendix IV.

10. *The immediate cause of the disaster*

10.1   The *HERALD* capsized because she went to sea with her inner and outer bow doors open. From the outset Mr. Mark Victor Stanley, who was the assistant bosun, has accepted that it was his duty to close the bow doors at the time of departure from Zeebrugge and that he failed to carry out this duty. Mr. Stanley had opened the bow doors on arrival in Zeebrugge. Thereafter he was engaged in supervising members of the crew in maintenance and cleaning the ship until he was released from work by the bosun, Mr. Ayling. Mr. Stanley then went to his cabin, where he fell asleep and was not awakened by the call "Harbour Stations", which was given over the Tannoy address system. He remained asleep on his bunk until he was thrown out of it when the *HERALD* began to capsize. Mr. Stanley has frankly recognised his failure to turn up for duty and he will, no doubt, suffer remorse for a long time to come. If the Company regards it as appropriate or necessary to take disciplinary action against Mr. Stanley it has power to do so under the Code of Conduct for the Merchant Navy. In fairness to Mr. Stanley it is right to record that after the *HERALD* capsized he found his way out of the ship on to her hull where he set about rescuing passengers trapped inside. He broke a window for access and, when he was scooping the glass away his right forearm was deeply cut. Nevertheless he re-entered the hull and went into the water to assist passengers. He continued until he was overcome by cold and bleeding.

10.2   The bosun, Mr. Terence Ayling, told the court that he thought he was the last man to leave G deck, where he had been working in the vicinity of the bow doors and that, so far as he knew, there was no one there to close the doors. He had put the chain across after the last car was loaded. There is no reason why the bow doors should not have been closed as soon as the chain was in position. Mr. Ayling was asked whether there was any reason why he should not have shut the doors. He replied "It has never been part of my duties to close the doors or make sure anybody is there to close the doors." He also said "At that stage it was harbour stations so everybody was going to their stations." He took a narrow view of his duties and it is most unfortunate that that was his attitude. It is only fair to add that his behaviour after the *HERALD* capsized was exemplary. In the absence of any deck officer he took the responsibility for organizing the rescue efforts, first from the bridge and later in the passenger spaces.

10.3   The questions which arise are: why was the absence of Mr. Stanley from his harbour station not noticed? and, why was there not a foolproof system which would ensure that the vital task of closing the bow doors was performed irrespective of the potential failure of any one individual? This was not the first occasion on which such a failure had occurred. In October 1983 the assistant bosun of the *PRIDE* had fallen asleep and had not heard "Harbour Stations" being called, with the result that he neglected to close both the bow and stern doors on the sailing of the vessel from No. 5 berth, Dover.

10.4   A general instruction issued in July 1984 prescribed that it was the duty of the officer loading the main vehicle deck (G deck) to ensure that the bow doors were "secure when leaving port". That instruction had been regularly flouted. It was interpreted as meaning that it was the duty of the loading officer merely to see that someone was at the controls and ready to close the doors. That is not the meaning of the instruction. The instruction is not clearly worded, but, whatever its precise meaning, it was not enforced. If it had been enforced this disaster would not have occurred. We will revert to these points later.

10.5   Mr. Paul Ronald Morter was the Second Officer of the *HERALD* on 6th March. Mr. Morter went to G deck during the course of loading to relieve the Chief Officer. Despite the arrival of Mr. Morter the Chief Officer remained on G deck for a time, without explaining why he did so. In due course the Chief Officer left Mr. Morter in charge of loading. About 10 or 15 minutes before the ship was due to sail the Chief Officer, who had overheard difficulties between Mr. Morter and the shore staff, returned and, according to a deposition made by him on the 1st April 1987, he suggested that the second officer should go aft and stand by for harbour stations while he completed the loading. That statement does not accord with the recollection of Mr. Morter. The evidence of Mr. Morter is that he did not expect the Chief

Officer to return before departure. When there were still 20 to 25 cars to load Mr. Morter overheard on his radio the Chief Officer giving orders. The two officers did not meet face to face. Mr. Morter assumed that once the Chief Officer had arrived and started issuing orders he, Mr. Morter, was no longer to exercise the responsibilities of loading officer. The Court sensed that there was some tension between the Chief Officer and Mr. Morter and that the whole picture had not emerged in the course of their evidence. We quote one short passage from the questions put to Mr. Morter by Mr. Owen and the answers thereto.

Q. Was there ever a set routine for loading this vessel?

A. The cargo duties were shared between the two officers on the ship, not in a set down pattern.

Q. On this occasion you were in effect relieved of responsibilities of the loading officer with a matter of minutes to go before sailing?

A. Yes.

Q. Was that unusual?

A. Yes

Q. When the Chief Officer came to G deck and started issuing orders did you regard yourself as relieved of any responsibility with regard to the closure of the bow doors on G deck?

A. I remained on G deck . . . He took over as loading officer so I assumed he took the responsibilities that go with that job.

Q. You say you assumed that, what was your understanding when that happened, did you think you were relieved of all responsibility to ensure that the bow doors were closed?

A. I was not sure, which was why I remained there and discussed it with the chief officer before I left the deck.

Q. Discussed the closing of the bow doors with him?

A. No.

Q. Well, what was it you were not sure about, whether you were still loading officer or what?

A. I knew that job had been taken away from me.

Q. What were you not sure about?

A. I discussed with the Chief Officer whether I would go aft, that was what I was clarifying with the Chief Officer, I was to go down aft.

Mr. Morter told the Court that if he had remained as the loading officer he would have communicated with the assistant bosun and he would have waited for a certain period and then chased after him.

10.6   Although the totality of the evidence left the Court with a sense of unease that the whole truth had not emerged, it was in the circumstances set out above that Mr. Leslie Sabel, the Chief Officer, relieved the Second Officer as loading officer of G deck shortly before he instructed the quartermaster to call the crew to harbour stations. Accordingly, it then became the duty of Mr. Sabel to ensure that the bow doors were closed. He does not dispute the fact that this was his duty. But he, too, interpreted the instruction laid down in July 1984 as a duty merely to ensure that the asssistant bosun was at the controls. Mr. Sabel had been working with Mr. Stanley during the day of the disaster and he knew that it was Mr. Stanley's duty to close the doors. Mr. Sabel should have been able to recognize Mr. Stanley.

10.7   The accuracy of some of the evidence given by Mr. Sabel was challenged at the Investigation. For this reason it is important to bear in mind the physical injuries and shock suffered by Mr. Sabel. When the *HERALD* began to heel to port, Mr. Sabel was in the officers' messroom. When he realised that something was seriously wrong he went to the bridge. He had entered the wheelhouse when the *HERALD* capsized. He lost his footing and was thrown violently to the port side. Water flooded into the wheelhouse and over his head. Mr. Sabel suffered injuries which were still causing him pain at the time when he was called as a witness to give oral evidence. The Court has made due allowance for his physical and mental condition.

10.8   The first recorded statement of Mr. Sabel was made in a deposition dated 1st April 1987. On that occasion he said:–

> "I then checked that there were no passengers in the bow area likely to come to harm, and ensured that there was a man standing by to close the bow doors, I do not remember who he was. Having ascertained everything was in order on the car deck, I went to the bridge, which was my harbour station, assisting the Master".

The evidence which Mr. Sabel gave at the Investigation was different. He then said that when he left G deck there was a man approaching, whom he thought was the assistant bosun coming to close the doors and that the man came within about 20 feet of him. His evidence was that there were passengers on the car deck (contrary to his earlier statement) and that he was distracted. If there was a man approaching, we know that the man was not the assistant bosun, who was asleep in his cabin. Who was it? Certainly it was not a member of the deck crew, all of whom were in other parts of the ship.

10.9   The body of one of the motormen was found on G deck after the *HERALD* had been salved. It seems highly unlikely that any man would have stayed on G deck for about 20 minutes while the *HERALD* put out to sea with her bow doors open. Therefore the presence of that body does not support the evidence of Mr. Sabel. As we have already said, Mr. Ayling thought he was the last man to leave G deck. The Court has reached the conclusion that Mr. Sabel's recollection as to what occurred is likely to be at fault. The probability is that he left the area of the bow doors at a time when there was no one on G deck. It is likely that at that time he felt under pressure to go to the bridge, because that was his harbour station, and that he had confidence that Mr. Stanley would arrive on G deck within a few moments. Mr. Sabel has carried out this operation on many occasions. When he was giving evidence he may have muddled one occasion with another. The precise facts are of no consequence because, on either version, Mr. Sabel failed to carry out his duty to ensure that the bow doors were closed. He was seriously negligent by reason of that failure. Of all the many faults which combined to lead directly or indirectly to this tragic disaster that of Mr. Leslie Sabel was the most immediate. This Court cannot condone such irresponsible conduct. For this reason his certificate of competency must be suspended.

11. *Pressure to leave the berth*

11.1   The Court found some difficulty in finding a clear answer to the question: Why could not the loading officer remain on G deck until the doors were closed before going to his harbour station on the bridge? That operation could be completed in less than three minutes. But the officers always felt under pressure to leave the berth immediately after the completion of loading. The practice was for the officer on the car deck to call the bridge and tell the quartermaster to give the order "harbour stations" over the Tannoy. Frequently the order "harbour stations" was given before loading was complete. The order was given as soon as the loading officer decided that by the time the crew arrived at their stations everything would be ready for the ship to proceed to sea. The evidence of Captain Lewry was that on the Zeebrugge run it would have been necessary to delay the order "harbour stations" until the bow doors had been closed if the Chief Officer was required to remain on G deck until this had been done.

11.2   The "Bridge and Navigational Procedures" guide which was issued by the Company included the following:

> Departure from Port
>
> a) O.O.W./Master should be on the Bridge approximately 15 minutes before the ship's sailing time; . . . . .

That order does not make it clear whether it was the duty of the O.O.W. or the Master to be on the bridge 15 mintues before sailing, or whether the officer was to remain on the bridge thereafter. If the O.O.W. was the loading officer, this order created a conflict in his duties. The conflict was brought to the attention of Mr. Develin by a memorandum dated 21st August 1982 from Captain Hackett, Senior Master of *FREE ENTERPRISE VIII* in which he said:–

> *Departure from Port*
>
> It is impractical for the O.O.W. (either the Chief or Second Officer) to be on the Bridge 15 minutes before sailing time. Both are fully committed to loading the ship. At sailing time, the Chief Officer stands by the bow or stern door to see the ramp out and assure papers are on board etc. The Second Officer proceeds to his after mooring station to assure that the propellers are clear and report to bridge.

The order illustrates the lack of thought given by management to the organisation of the officers' duties.

11.3   The sense of urgency to sail at the earliest possible moment was exemplified by an internal memorandum sent to assistant managers by Mr. D. Shipley, who was the operations manager at Zeebrugge. It is dated 18th August 1986 and the relevant parts of it reads as follows:

> "There seems to be a general tendency of satisfaction if the ship has sailed two or three minutes early. Where, a full load is present, then every effort has to be made to sail the ship 15 minutes earlier . . . . . I expect to read from now onwards, especially where FE8 is concerned, that the ship left 15 minutes early . . . . . put pressure on the first officer if you don't think he is moving fast enough. Have your load ready when the vessel is in and marshall your staff and machines to work efficiently. Let's put the record straight, sailing late out of Zeebrugge isn't on. It's 15 minutes early for us."

Mr. A. P. Young sought to explain away that memorandum on the basis that the language was used merely for purposes of what he called "motivation". But it was entirely in keeping with his own thoughts at that time. On the 13th August 1986 Captain Thorne, the Senior Master of *FREE ENTERPRISE VIII*, sent a memorandum to Deck Officers with a copy to Mr. Young, in which he said:–

> "Finally, one of the reasons for such late arrivals is due to late departures from Dover the cause of which is rarely due to any inefficiency on the port of Dover staff – just lack of time available to handle both discharge and loading together with storing (often only 30–40 minutes). This situation can often be assisted by an early sailing from Zeebrugge the previous voyage: Zeebrugge staff MUST be made aware of such necessity immediately upon arrival".

Mr. Young replied:–

> "I would just like to state that I thoroughly endorse your action".

The Court was left in no doubt that deck officers felt that there was no time to be wasted. The Company sought to say that this disaster could have been avoided if the Chief Officer had waited on G deck another three minutes. That is true. But the Company took no proper steps to ensure that the Chief Officer remained on G deck until the bow doors were closed. On the 6th March they were running late. The *HERALD* sailed 5 minutes late. This may have contributed to Mr. Sabel's decision to leave G deck before the arrival of Mr. Stanley, which he anticipated.

12. *Captain David Lewry*

12.1   Captain Lewry was Master of the *HERALD* on the 6th March 1987. In that capacity he was responsible for the safety of his ship and every person on board. Captain Lewry took the *HERALD* to sea with the bow doors fully open, with the consequences which have been related. It follows that Captain Lewry must accept personal responsibility for the loss of his ship.

12.2   In judging his conduct it is right to look at it in perspective. Captain Lewry has served at sea for over 30 years. He has held a Master's Certificate of Competency (Foreign Going) for over 20 years, and he has been in command of a ship for 10 years.

12.3   Captain Lewry joined the *HERALD* on 13th March 1980 as one of five masters. The Company has issued a set of standing orders which included the following:—

> "01.09 *Ready for Sea*
>
> Heads of Departments are to report to the Master immediately they are aware of any deficiency which is likely to cause their departments to be unready for sea in any respect at the due sailing time.
>
> In the absence of any such report the Master will assume, at the due sailing time, that the vessel is ready for sea in all respects".

That order was unsatisfactory in many respects. It followed immediately after 01.08 which was an order that defects had to be reported to the Head of Department. The sequence of orders raises at least a suspicion that the draftsman used the word 'deficiency' in 01.09 as synonymous with 'defect' in 01.08. On one construction of the orders, order 01.09 was merely completing the process of ensuring that the Master was apprised of all defects. That is how this Court would have interpreted it. But it appears that that is not the way in which order 01.09 was interpreted by deck officers. Masters came to rely upon the absence of any report at the time of sailing as satisfying them that their ship was ready for sea in all respects. That was, of course, a very dangerous assumption.

12.4   On the 6th March, Captain Lewry saw the Chief Officer come to the Bridge. Captain Lewry did not ask him if the ship was all secure and the Chief Officer did not make a report. Captain Lewry was entitled to assume that the assistant bosun and the Chief Officer were qualified to perform their respective duties, but he should not have assumed that they had done so. He should have insisted upon receiving a report to that effect.

12.5   In mitigation of Captain Lewry's failure to ensure that his ship was in all respects ready for sea a number of points were made on his behalf, of which the three principal ones were as follows. First, Captain Lewry merely followed a system which was operated by all the masters of the *HERALD* and approved by the Senior Master, Captain Kirby. Second, the court was reminded that the orders entitled "Ship's standing orders" issued by the Company make no reference, as they should have done, to opening and closing the bow and stern doors. Third, before this disaster there had been no less than five occasions when one of the Company's ships had proceeded to sea with bow or stern doors open. Some of those incidents were known to the management, who had not drawn them to the attention of the other Masters. Captain Lewry told the Court that if he had been made aware of any of those incidents he would have instituted a new system under which he would have required a report that the doors were closed. It is possible that he would have done so. But those Masters who were aware of the occasions when ships proceeded to sea with bow or stern doors open did not change their orders. The Court has borne in mind all the points which were made on behalf of Captain Lewry.

12.6 The system which was in operation in all the Spirit class ships was defective. The fact that other Masters operated the same defective system does not relieve Catain Lewry of his personal responsibility for taking his ship to sea in an unsafe condition. In so doing he was seriously negligent in the discharge of his duties. That negligence was one of the causes contributing to the casualty. The Court is aware of the mental and emotional burden resulting from this disaster which has been and will be borne by Captain Lewry, but the Court would be failing in its duty if it did not suspend his Certificate of Competency.

13. *Captain John Michael Kirby*

13.1 Captain Kirby was one of the five masters who took it in turn to command the *HERALD*. He was the Senior Master as from May 1985. One of his functions as Senior Master was to act as a co-ordinator between all the masters and officers of the ship in order to achieve uniformity in the practices operated by the different crews. As three different crews served with five different sets of officers, it was essential that there should be uniformity of practice. Furthermore there were frequent changes amongst the officers. Captain Kirby drew attention to this in an internal memorandum dated 22nd November 1986 and addressed to Mr. M. Ridley, Chief Superintendent. Parts of that memorandum must be quoted:

> "The existing system of Deck Officer manning for the 'Blue Riband Class', ship which relieves on the Zeebrugge run is unsatisfactory. When '*HERALD*' took up the Zeebrugge service our Deck Officers were reduced from the usual complement of 15 to 10. The surplus 5 were distributed round the fleet. On '*HERALD'S*' return to the Calais service, instead of our own Officers returning to the ship, we were and are being manned by officers from whichever ship is at refit. Due to this system, together with Trainee Master moves, '*HERALD*' will have had a total of exactly 30 different deck officers on the books during the period 29th September 1986 to 5th January 1987 . . . . Many of the transient officers are only here for a few duties and in these circumstances their main concern is to get the ship loaded and safely between Dover and Calais. Although they are generally good officers it is unrealistic to expect them to become involved in the checking of installations and equipment or the detailed organisation of this particular vessel which they do not regard as their own . . . ."

Captain Kirby returned to this theme with a further memorandum dated 28th January 1987 which was also addressed to Mr. Ridley. In that memorandum he said:

> "I wish to stress again that *HERALD* badly needs a *permanent* complement of good deck officers. Our problem was outlined in my memo of 22nd November. Since then the throughput of officers has increased even further, partly because of sickness. During the period from 1st September 1986 to 28th January 1987 a total of 36 deck officers have been attached to the ship. We have also lost two masters (Hammond and Irving) and gained one (Robinson). To make matters worse the vessel has had an unprecedented seven changes in sailing schedule. The result has been a serious loss in continuity. Shipboard maintenance, safety gear checks, crew training and the overall smooth running of the vessel have all suffered . . ."

A list of the 36 officers referred to in the memorandum, was appended.

13.2 For the *HERALD* Captain Kirby adopted a set of General Instructions issued by a Captain Martin in July 1984. He was satisfied with them and accepted them as his own. Those instructions included the following:-

> "2. The officer loading the main vehicle deck, G Deck, to ensure that the water tight and bow/stern doors are secured when leaving port."

Captain Kirby was content that there had been sufficient compliance with that instruction if the loading officer ensured that the assistant bosun was actually at the control position and (apparently) going to operate the doors before the officer left to go to his own harbour station. That was not compliance with the Instructions "to *ensure* that the bow doors were secured". As the Senior Master did not enforce compliance with that very important instruction, he could not expect other masters to do so.

13.3 But not only did Captain Kirby fail to enforce such orders as had been promulgated, he also failed to issue clear and concise orders about the closing of the most important doors on G deck. He should have introduced a fail-safe system. Furthermore, he was content to accept without demur the Ship's Standing Orders issued by the Company. For reasons which we will set out later those orders are not clear or adequate. As the Senior Master and as an experienced Master, Captain Kirby ought to have applied his mind to the contents of those Orders. If he had done so he would certainly have appreciated their defects. Captain Kirby was one of many masters who failed to apply their minds to those Orders and to take steps to have them clarified. Captain Kirby must bear his share of the responsibility for the disaster.

14. *The Management*

14.1 At first sight the faults which led to this disaster were the aforesaid errors of omission on the part of the Master, the Chief Officer and the assistant bosun, and also the failure by Captain Kirby to issue and enforce clear orders. But a full investigation into the circumstances of the disaster leads inexorably to the conclusion that the underlying or cardinal faults lay higher up in the Company. The Board of Directors did not appreciate their responsibility for the safe management of their ships. They did not apply their minds to the question: What orders should be given for the safety of our ships? The directors did not have any proper comprehension of what their duties were. There appears to have been a lack of thought about the way in which the *HERALD* ought to have been organised for the Dover/Zeebrugge run. All concerned in management, from the members of the Board of Directors down to the junior superintendents, were guilty of fault in that all must be regarded as sharing responsibility for the failure of management. From top to bottom the body corporate was infected with the disease of sloppiness. This became particularly apparent from the evidence of Mr A. P. Young, who was the Operations Director and Mr. W. J. Ayers, who was Technical Director. As will become apparent from later passages in this Report, the Court was singularly unimpressed by both these gentlemen. The failure on the part of the shore management to give proper and clear directions was a contributory cause of the disaster. This is a serious finding which must be explained in some detail.

14.2 In July 1986 the Department issued Merchant Shipping Notice No. M. 1188 entitled "Good Ship Management". The advice given in that Notice included the following points:

> "The efficient and safe operation of ships requires the exercise of good management both at sea and ashore . . . . The overall responsibility of the shipping company requires the need for close involvement by management ashore. To this end it is recommended that every company operating ships should designate a person ashore with responsibility for monitoring the technical and safety aspects of

the operation of its ships and for providing appropriate shore based back-up . . . . Stress is placed upon the importance of providing the Master with clear instructions to him and his officers. The instructions should include adequate Standing Orders. There should be close co-operation and regular and effective communication in both directions between ship and shore."

That is very sound advice. It is advice which ought to have been unnecessary. A well-run ship-owning Company should have been organized in that manner before receiving the Notice. Mr. Develin was aware of that Notice. He thought that the Company Structure, its attitude to the Masters and its instructions complied with that advice. When he saw the Notice he took no action on it. It is only necessary to quote one example of how the standard of management fell short of the recommendations contained in that Notice. It reveals a staggering complacency.

On the 18th March 1986 there was a meeting of senior Masters with management, at which Mr. Develin was in the Chair. One of the topics raised for discussion concerned the recognition of the Chief Officer as Head of Department and the roles of the Maintenance Master and Chief Officer. Mr. Develin said, although he was still considering writing definitions of these different roles, he felt "it was more preferable not to define the roles but to allow them to evolve". That attitude was described by Mr. Owen, with justification, as an abject abdication of responsibility. It demonstrates an inability or unwillingness to give clear orders. **Clear instructions are the foundation of a safe system of operation.** It was the failure to give clear orders about the duties of the Officers on the Zeebrugge run which contributed so greatly to the causes of this disaster. Mr. Clarke, on behalf of the Company, said that it was not the responsibility of Mr. Develin to see that the Company orders were properly drafted. In answer to the question, "Who was responsible?" Mr. Clarke said "Well in truth, nobody, though there ought to have been". The Board of Directors must accept a heavy responsibility for their lamentable lack of directions. Individually and collectively they lacked a sense of responsibility. This left, what Mr. Owen so aptly described as, "a vacuum at the centre".

14.3   In the course of this Investigation other failures on the part of the management, which were not causative of the casualty, emerged in the evidence. Although they did not contribute to the disaster they are symptomatic of the malaise which infected the Company and they are matters of public concern. Lessons can be learned from them which may be useful to all operators of passenger ferries of similar type.

14.4   As there are lengthy passages in this Report in which there is criticism of the management of the Company, it is only fair to the Company to state at this stage that a new Chairman took office only a short time before the disaster and much has been done since to improve the Company's approach to ship management. The Court was very favourably impressed by the evidence of Mr. J.F. Ford, the new Chairman, and that of Mr. A.D. Barratt, a director and general manager. We will make further mention of this evidence later in this Report, but we mention it at this stage for the benefit of those who do not read to the end of the Report.

14.5   It is also right to say that the Company has recognised its causative faults. On the eighth day of this Investigation Mr. Clarke said "Townsend Car Ferries recognise that long before the 6th March 1987 both their sea and shore staff should have given proper consideration to the adequacy of the whole system relating to the closing of doors on this class of ship with their clam doors. If they had, they should, and would, have improved the system notably by first improving their instructions, at the very least by introducing in the Bridge and Navigation Procedures Guide an express instruction that the doors should be closed, secondly by introducing a positive reporting system, thirdly by ensuring that the closure of the doors was properly checked and, fourthly, by introducing a monitoring or checking system". That was a helpful and realistic statement.

15. *Standing Orders*

15.1   The Company issued to the *HERALD* a document entitled "SHIP'S STANDING ORDERS". As these orders were issued by the Company it would have been clearer if they had been entitled "COMPANY STANDING ORDERS", in order to distinguish them from standing orders issued by the Senior Master or by the Head of a Department. The first section contains general orders. The first of those general orders is in the following terms:–

> "01.01 *Departmental Orders*
>
> For administrative purposes the ship will be organised into four main departments: Deck, Radio, Engineering and Catering. The heads of these departments are each to prepare and issue a set of Standing Orders covering the organisation and working of their departments. They are to be in looseleaf form to facilitate amendment. These orders are to be approved and countersigned by the Senior Master."

After quoting that order Mr. Steel asked Captain Lewry "Now, the Court would like to know who did you understand to be the head of the deck department?" Captain Lewry replied "It depends in which context the expression is being used. The head of the deck department on day to day running of the ship was the Chief Officer." The next question was "Well, who in the context of issuing Standing Orders was head of the department?" Captain Lewry replied "I issued orders as to work routines for the deck department ratings, POs, Quartermasters, Carpenters, so as far as working routines were concerned I was the head of the deck department."

15.2   **Any set of orders must be so drafted that every expression therein has only one meaning throughout those orders.** There would have been no difficulty in using the expression "Chief Officer" whenever he was referred to, or "The Master" if the order referred to him.

15.3   In the context of the matters under investigation, the worst features of the Standing Orders were (1) they made no reference to closing the bow and stern doors, and (2) they appear to have led Captain Lewry to assume that his ship was ready for sea in all respects merely because he had had no report to the contrary. Order number 01.09, upon which Captain Lewry relied, has already been quoted in this Report, and we have referred in paragraph 7.4 above to an absence of thought as to how the *HERALD* should have been organised for the Dover/Zeebrugge run. In addition to the differences between the Calais and Zeebrugge runs, there is another factor to be taken into consideration. Some ferries are built with vizor doors which, when open, can be seen from the bridge. Accordingly in such ships the Master always knows whether the vizor door is open or closed. When the Spirit class ships were built with clam doors it appears not to have crossed the mind of any manager to include in the Standing Orders an order that the closure of those doors must be reported to the bridge and recorded in the log book.

16. *The lack of a Marine Superintendent*

16.1   The questions which the Court has been asked to answer include: what lessons can be learned from the practices relating to the embarkation of passengers and the loading of freight and preparing the *HERALD* for sea? To answer those questions the Court must look first at the organisation of the Company ashore.

16.2   Mr. Develin became a Chief Engineer in 1966. He joined the Company in May 1975. In 1978 he became known as the "Chief Marine Superintendent" and in 1986 he became a director of the Company. When he became a director his successor was appointed "Chief Superintendent", omitting the word "Marine" because Mr. Develin rightly thought that the former title was misleading in the industry. Mr. Develin was pepared to accept that he was responsible for the safe operation of the Company's ships. Another director, Mr. Ayers, told the Court that no director was solely responsible for safety. Mr. Develin thought that before

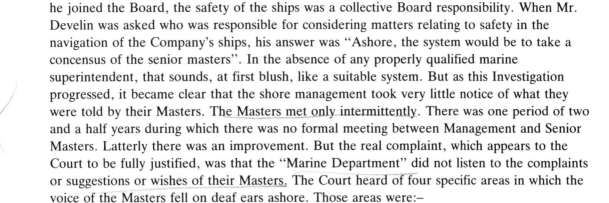

he joined the Board, the safety of the ships was a collective Board responsibility. When Mr. Develin was asked who was responsible for considering matters relating to safety in the navigation of the Company's ships, his answer was "Ashore, the system would be to take a concensus of the senior masters". In the absence of any properly qualified marine superintendent, that sounds, at first blush, like a suitable system. But as this Investigation progressed, it became clear that the shore management took very little notice of what they were told by their Masters. The Masters met only intermittently. There was one period of two and a half years during which there was no formal meeting between Management and Senior Masters. Latterly there was an improvement. But the real complaint, which appears to the Court to be fully justified, was that the "Marine Department" did not listen to the complaints or suggestions or wishes of their Masters. The Court heard of four specific areas in which the voice of the Masters fell on deaf ears ashore. Those areas were:–

(a) Complaints that ships proceeded to sea carrying passengers in excess of the permitted number.

(b) The wish to have lights fitted on the bridge to indicate whether the bow and stern doors were open or closed.

(c) Draught marks could not be read. Ships were not provided with instruments for reading draughts. At times ships were required to arrive and sail from Zeebrugge trimmed by the head, without any relevant stability information.

(d) The wish to have a high capacity ballast pump to deal with the Zeebrugge trimming ballast.

Each of these matters must be dealt with in turn.

17. *Carriage of excessive numbers of passengers*

17.1   The stability information book published on the 28th May 1980 and approved by the Department gives some general particulars of the ship and states that in the C2 condition up to a draught of 5.5 m moulded the ship may carry 1,400 passengers and crew, but thereafter if loaded up to the C1 draught of 5.7 m moulded the ship could carry only 630 passengers and crew.

17.2   During the course of the evidence it became apparent from the documents that there were no less than seven different Masters, each of whom found that from time to time his ship was carrying passengers substantially in excess of the permitted number. The documents reveal the following state of affairs.

17.3   The Senior Master of *PRIDE OF FREE ENTERPRISE*, Captain Blowers, sent a memorandum dated 16.8.82 to Mr A. P. Young, who was the Operations Director, with a copy to Mr. Develin. The relevant passages from that memorandum are these:–

> *"Passenger Numbers*
>
> I have to report that on several occasions in the past two weeks the vessel is believed to have been carrying passengers in excess of our passenger limit i.e. 1,305. Examples I have details of are as follows:–
>
> 1. 28.7.82 1200 Dover/Calais – excess of some 250 passengers.
>
> 2. 6.8.82 1200 Dover/Calais – excess of some 40 passengers.
>
> 3. 8.8.82 1515 Calais/Dover – excess of some 100 passengers.
>
> 4. 15.8.82 1515 Calais/Dover – excess of some 171 passengers.

I attach a copy of a memo from one of the assistant bosuns in respect of the first three examples above together with a copy of the Manifest referred to. In respect of example 4 which was yesterday, the discrepancy seems to have occurred over the foot passengers numbering 225 for which no details were received.

In view of recent disquiet on this subject, the Master on duty last Saturday decided on making a ship's count as there was a maximum load booked. The duty manager ashore was informed as a matter of course. It was the impression of those ships' staff concerned that in view of the above that there was increased activity on behalf of those responsible for the shore count and that the two totals tallied fairly well – shore count = 1,260, ship count = 1,275, tickets = 1,270.

With respect to the above, and apart from the obvious moralities and swingeing penalties involved, I am most deeply concerned lest idle gossip, perhaps emanating from the Purser's office where they are faced with the details before they arise, should find its way to the media with all the damaging enquiries that would follow."

Mr. Young replied on 24th August 1982 with a memorandum to Captain Blowers in which he said:

"Frankly I am amazed and annoyed that personnel on board your vessel formed the opinion that because of their presence there was more activity in the passenger count. Do they really believe that shore personnel adopt a thoroughly irresponsible attitude to the serious subject of passenger limitations and counts. If they do they are totally out of order and you are ill-informed. Time and again we have made it quite clear that the counting of numbers of passengers on tickets may not agree with the actual head count for a varying number of reasons. The most recent example being on a Calais/Dover sailing when a ticket showing 191 passengers was included in a particular ship's document although the passengers had travelled on the sailing before. Steps have been taken to ensure that if such an incident occurs on any future occasion, the vessel's Purser that is actually carrying the ticket is to be notified so that although he would include the correct count on our internal ticket audit forms, he would give the head count for all over purposes. Your point regarding idle gossip, perhaps emanating from the Purser's office, is taken but surely the correct education of the facts to such persons will go some way to rectifying this situation and hence I feel that Masters and Officers could assist, instead of their continual disbelief in the intentions and abilities of shore based staff."

17.4   On 31st October 1982 Captain Pearson, who was Master of the *SPIRIT OF FREE ENTERPRISE* wrote a memorandum to Mr. Young in which he said:–

"I feel I must bring to your attention that on two sailings on Friday last, the 0900 D/C, and the 2015 C/D sailings, according to ticket count, the vessel was on these two occasions over her passenger limit.

Whilst accepting all the inherent difficulties of counting heads and tickets, it appears that commercial drivers were excluded from the shore count.

The crew complement for the day was 81, giving a passenger maximum of 1,319.

18

1. 0900 D/C. Shore count manifested was 1,319, the Purser's ticket count gave 1,364, an excess of 45.

2. 2015 C/D. Shore count manifested was 1,286, the Purser's ticket count gave 1,343, an excess of 57.

It may well be coincidental, but it appears that on both sailings the excesses were equal to the number of commercial drivers, giving the impression that they are being discounted from the total, which of course should not be so. To this end perhaps you would investigate the matter at your ealiest convenience, and may I add that of course the manifested figure, was that required."

17.5   Mr. Young wrote to Mr A.W. Cole on 3rd November 1982 in the following terms:–

"*Re: Excess Passenger Numbers*
S.O.F.E. – 29.10.82

Will you please find enclosed, herewith, copy of a memorandum I have received from Captain J. Pearson.

It does appear that on each occasion numbers of freight drivers were not included in the passenger figure given to the vessel and I think I would ask you to ensure that those concerned are made aware of the error and told to take more care in the future.

For information it is still my intention to eventually retain all tickets ashore, which will cut out the differences between head count and ticket count, but it will in no way lessen the need to be absolutely accurate at all times."

The last paragraph of that letter seems to suggest that by retaining all tickets ashore it would not be possible for those in the purser's office on board to find out whether there was a discrepancy between the number of tickets sold and the number of passengers carried.

17.6   The matter was discussed at a meeting between Senior Masters and shore management on 9th December 1982 at which Mr. Develin took the chair. The minutes of that meeting include the following passage:

"*Passenger Counts*

Captain Morgan raised the question of the inaccuracy of passenger counts, pointing out that some passengers, e.g. those under 4 years of age, could get on board without tickets.

Mr. Young replied that this was why head counts were taken, but even these were not totally accurate. Four counts were made – cars, coaches, freight and foot passengers and these figures were used to adjust the load. Tickets were taken on board and then counted, but for various reasons they invariably did not tally with the head count. Next year it was proposed to alter the system so that tickets were not taken on board, but instead retained ashore and counted. It would mean more staff ashore and still no guarantee that the numbers would be totally accurate. Captain Morgan asked if the vessels would know the passenger numbers. Mr. Young answered "yes – the numbers would be declared on the manifest, as was done at present." Captain Martin was concerned as to how to identify parties of passengers without having access to the tickets and Captain Elsom forecast problems if there was no declaration to the ship regarding the numbers of passengers on board. Mr. Young answered that the manifest provided the answers. He believed the head count, although not totally accurate, gave the best indication as to numbers."

Thus in 1982 there was good reason for thinking that ships in the Company's fleet were on occasions carrying passengers substantially in excess of their permitted number and that the legitimate complaints made by the Masters were not well received by Mr. Young. His statement that the manifest provided the answers has a hollow ring when it is compared with what he said in 1986.

17.7   In May 1983 and in March 1984 ship-Masters were again directing the attention of the management to their concern over excessive numbers of passengers. But the matter became really serious in 1986. The Court heard evidence from Captain de Ste Croix, who was Master of the *PRIDE OF FREE ENTERPRISE*. On the 1st August 1986 he sent a memorandum to Mr. Young which will be quoted in full:

> "Passenger Numbers on 1500 D/C, 1.8.86
>
> On the above sailing from Dover, the first passenger total given to the RO by the Purser was 1288. A call from the manifest office then informed the RO to add on another 214. The RO queried this as the total then had been way over the top. After a short delay the manifest office came back with a figure of 1014 plus an add-on of 214 making a total of 1228.
>
> As seeds of doubt had by then been sown in my mind I decided to have a head count as they went off to Calais. The following figures were revealed.

Foot passengers of skywalk	—	53 pax*
Coaches off top deck	—	742 pax (15 coaches)
Cars off top deck	—	265 pax
Coaches off bottom deck	—	320 pax (6 coaches)
Cars off bottom deck	—	179 pax
Freight off bottom deck	—	14 pax
Sale and save	—	10 pax
Total		1587 pax
Crew		95 pax
Total on board		1682

> This total is way over the life saving capacity of the vessel. The fine on the Master for this offence is £50,000 and probably confiscation of certificate. May I please know what steps the company intend to take to protect my career from the mistakes of this nature."

> (N.B. *pax means passengers)

17.8   On the 15th August 1986 Captain Stoker, Master of the *PRIDE* wrote:

> "*Passenger Figures*
>
> Because of recent discrepancies in the passenger count from Dover, I carried out a count during the off-loading in Calais of today's 1500 hours sailing from Dover."

Captain Stoker then set out the figures which showed an excess of 29 and he finished the letter with the words — "May I ask that you and your staff urgently look at your current methods and either make them work or amend as necessary."

17.9   On the 30th August 1986 Captain Martin, who was Senior Master of the *SPIRIT* sent a memorandum to Mr. Young and Mr. Develin calling attention to the fact that on one voyage a head count at Calais revealed that 1550 persons had been carried on the voyage. He added:

> "Making due allowance for discrepancies on both counts, the number of passengers over and above our certified number is clearly not unacceptable and can only be described as a blatant and flagrant disregard of the system, and backs up other complaints from Masters of this and other fleet vessels."

Captain Martin asked for an assurance that immediate steps would be taken to remind shore staff of their responsibilities.

On the 19th August 1986 Mr Young replied to Captain Stoker with the words:

> "I accept that the present method of obtaining the correct number of passengers boarding vessels is liable to error but I feel that everyone must accept that whatever system is operated there will always be the possibility of human error. However, please be assured that we shall fully discuss our current methods to eliminate any loopholes or shortcomings that exist so that we may continue to provide what, in the main, has come to mean a reliable and responsible system of passenger counting, bearing in mind the geography of both the vessels and shore approaches to the vessels and the limited in-port times, which even if we extend would not guarantee a 100% correct count."

17.10   On the 12th September 1986 Captain Hartwell of the *PRIDE* drew attention to a further substantial difference between the figures given and the total carried. He added:

> "Although not exceeding our passenger limit, I need not point out how serious this large discrepancy could be in an emergency to our integrity and efficiency if this sort of situation became public. Of course errors can occur but they are becoming so frequent it is almost being treated as a joke by those who inevitably get to know on board, and is positively embarrassing."

On the 16th September 1986 Mr. Cole sent a memorandum to all assistant managers telling them that they must exercise greater control over those who are obviously at present not completing their duties in a satisfactory manner. He said it is obviously imperative that greater attention is given by the loading staff to ensure that the count is more accurate than has been seen to be the case on a number of occasions.

17.11   On the 19th September 1986 Captain Ferrier of the *PRIDE* wrote to Mr. Young. He said that once again he had to report that the vessel was overloaded leaving Dover. He drew attention to an excess of 72 passengers.

On the 29th September 1986 Captain Martin again wrote to Mr. Young drawing attention to the fact that on the Calais/Dover run he had carried an excess of 200 passengers.

On the 28th October 1986 the Senior Master of *FREE ENTERPRISE IV* wrote a memorandum to Mr. Young drawing attention to the fact that on the 18th October the ship was grossly overloaded. He asked for an asssurance that there would be a proper review of the system for counting heads.

17.12   Mr. Cole's answer dated 29th October 1986 is illuminating. He said: "I refer to your memo of 28/10/86 addressed to Mr. Young re alleged overloading in particular with the voyage 0930 Dover/Boulogne Saturday 18/10/86." He said that he confirmed that the figure of 1067 was correct "but some stray tickets, that had to be put into the system somewhere, had in fact been added to that sailing which produced a false figure of 1200." Mr. Young was asked about that statement. **At first his answers were very evasive, but eventually he agreed that the figure given in the manifest was a false figure.**

On the 31st October 1986 Mr. Develin sent a memorandum to Mr. Young in the following terms:

> "*Passenger figures*
>
> I refer in particular to Captain Davenport's memo of 28th October 1986 and Mr. A.W. Cole's reply of 29th October 1986. Also I refer generally to several memos from various Masters on this subject and finally, to discussion in recent Senior Masters' meetings, again on this subject.
>
> In view of the serious nature of this matter, and the fact that we must get it right and, also, be seen to be getting it right by the Masters, so that they may have total confidence in the system, think it is necessary that we look at the subject in detail.
>
> With this in view, I would suggest that either yourself or A.W. Cole (or indeed both of you) meet with Captain Davenport (representing the Senior Masters) and myself to achieve same.
>
> My secretary will telephone in due course to book a suitably convenient date."

Mr. Young did not invite Mr. Develin to meet him to discuss this subject. Mr. Young took the view that this was not a marine matter and deliberately excluded Mr. Develin from further investigation of the problem.

17.13   Captain Hartwell again made a complaint on the 8th November 1986 when his count disclosed that the *PRIDE* had been carrying 1342 passengers and 100 crew. It was said that the excess of passengers were carried unintentionally.

Mr. Young was unwilling to accept the figures given to him by no less than seven Masters. Mr. Young accepted the view that a head count was the most accurate way of determining how many persons were on board. He also accepted that if a head count was made rapidly it was likely that any error would have come about by missing a few passengers. In that event the total number actually carried would have been even more than the number disclosed by the head count.

17.14   **The Court reluctantly concluded that Mr. Young made no proper or sincere effort to solve the problem.** The Court takes a most serious view of the fact that so many of the Company's ferries were carrying an excessive number of passengers on so many occasions. Not only was it illegal for the excess passengers to have been carried, but also it was dangerous. It should not have been beyond the wit of the managers to devise a system which would have ensured that no more than the permitted number of passengers are carried.

17.15   After it became apparent that this Court was greatly interested in the system for checking the number of passengers carried on each ship further thought was given to this matter by the Company. On the 29th May 1987 Mr. A.P. Young produced a memorandum containing some ideas for improving the system of counting the number of passengers. Those ideas include the introduction of a boarding card system for passengers who do not arrive in vehicles. **The Court considers that it would be possible to introduce a system under which every passenger has a boarding card.** The number of boarding cards issued for each voyage would correspond with the maximum number of passengers which can legitimately be carried, which would automatically avoid the risk of carrying excess passengers. The Court can only express the hope that whatever system is introduced it will be effective in ensuring that the number of passengers carried does not exceed the permitted number.

17.16   There is another aspect of the number of passengers carried which disturbed the Court, and that is whether there was any serious attempt to restrict the number of persons on board to 630 when the draught exceeded 5.5 m, or to ensure that the draught did not exceed 5.5 m if more than 550 passengers were embarked. Despite the evidence of Mr. Ayers that it was not possible for the officers to read the draught marks, and the evidence of Captain Lewry that no attempt was made to read the draught, Mr. Young told the Court that the shore staff relied on the ship's officers to ensure that the ship was not overloaded. He said:

> "The officers inspect the loadline and the shore staff rely on that. I must add that the guide we have is a guide from the ships to give us a possibility of organizing a load on their behalf. Having commenced the loading which is under the instruction of the ship's officer, the shore staff will continue sending traffic to the vessel until told not to do so, because the shore personnel expect the ship's officer to halt as he sees necessary any traffic coming to the ship."

In fact the loading officers did not tell the shore staff to stop sending vehicles to the ship. They did not know the draught of their ship. The Court regards that as a serious deficiency.

18. Indicator lights

18.1   Whenever the HERALD was at sea her safety depended upon the bow and stern doors being closed and properly secured. Not only should those doors have been closed on every occasion before the HERALD left her berth, but also the mechanism for opening the doors should have been secured in a manner which could prevent anyone from re-opening the doors until an order to do so had been given.

18.2   On the 29th October 1983 the assistant bosun of the PRIDE neglected to close both the bow and stern doors on sailing from No. 5 berth Dover. It appears that he had fallen asleep and, for that reason, he failed to carry out that duty.

18.3   On the 6th October 1984 the Master of the PRIDE sent a circular to all deck officers, bosuns and assistant bosuns in the following terms:

> "Twice since going on the Zeebrugge run, this ship has sailed with the stern or bow doors open. No doubt this is caused by job/rank changes from the Calais run, however all those named persons must see that the system is worked to make sure this dangerous situation does not occur. Give it your utmost attention."

18.4   On the 28th June 1985 Captain Blowers of the PRIDE wrote a sensible memorandum to Mr. Develin. The relevant parts of the memorandum are these:

> "In the hope that there might be one or two ideas worthy of consideration I am forwarding some points that have been suggested on this ship and with reference to any future new-building programme. Many of the items are mentioned because of the excessive amounts of maintenance, time and money spent on them."

> "4. Mimic Panel – There is no indication on the bridge as to whether the most important watertight doors are closed or not. That is the bow or stern doors. With the very short distance between the berth and the open sea on both sides of the channel this can be a problem if the operator is delayed or having problems in closing the doors. Indicator lights on the very excellent mimic panel could enable the bridge team to monitor the situation in such circumstances."

On the 10th July 1985 Mr. Develin replied, saying that he would pass the comments to Tonbridge for their 'think-tank', and thanking "all concerned for their obvious effort in compiling these details."

18.5   Mr. Develin circulated that memorandum amongst managers for comment. It was a serious memorandum which merited serious thought and attention, and called for a considered reply. The answers which Mr. Develin received will be set out verbatim. From Mr. J.F. Alcindor, a deputy chief superintendent: "Do they need an indicator to tell them whether the deck storekeeper is awake and sober? My goodness!!" From Mr. A.C. Reynolds: "Nice but don't we already pay someone!" From Mr. R. Ellison: "Assume the guy who shuts the doors tells the bridge if there is a problem." From Mr. D.R. Hamilton: "Nice!" It is hardly necessary for the Court to comment that these replies display an absence of any proper sense of responsibility. Moreover the comment of Mr. Alcindor on the deck storekeeper was either ominously prescient or showed an awareness of this type of incident in the past. **If the sensible suggestion that indicator lights be installed had received, in 1985, the serious consideration which it deserved, it is at least possible that they would have been fitted in the early months of 1986 and this disaster might well have been prevented.**

18.6   The matter was raised again in 1986 by Captain Kirby and Captain de Ste Croix. On the 17th May 1986 Captain J. Kirby, the Senior Master of *HERALD*, wrote a memorandum to Mr. Alcindor on the subject of improvements to the "SPIRIT class" wheelhouse layout. Those suggestions included: "17. Bow and stern doors. Open/closed indication to be duplicated on bridge."

18.7   On the 9th October 1986 Captain de Ste Croix sent a memorandum to the Senior Electrical Officer in the following terms:

> "Ron
> Another incident has occurred to remind me of my request of some time ago for bridge indication of the position of the bow and stern watertight doors.
>
> I still feel that although it is the duty of a crew member to check the position of the doors visually prior to proceeding to sea, it is so important to the safety of the ship that they are closed that we should have bridge indication. We have indicators for many pieces of equipment on the bridge, many of which should be checked visually in another part of the ship e.g. main engine bridge stands connected, bow thrusts on the board etc., and I feel that the bow and stern doors are every bit as important as these. Is the issue still being considered or has it been considered too difficult or expensive?"

On that memorandum was written:

> "Tony
> Please submit request to marine department on the usual application form. If it receives their blessing I will proceed with the specification. It can be done, but will require a few deck and bulkhead penetrations."

On the 13th October 1986 Captain de Ste Croix submitted a job specification for modifications in these terms:

> "Bridge indication is required to show whether the G deck bow and stern w/t doors are in the secure or insecure mode."

On this specification Mr. Alcindor wrote:

"Please write up preliminary specification for pricing."

On the 18th October 1986 Mr. R.W. King sent a memorandum to Mr. Alcindor in which he said:

"I cannot see the purpose or the need for the stern door to be monitored on the bridge, as the seaman in charge of closing the doors is standing by the control panel watching them close."

On the 21st October 1986 Mr. Alcindor sent a memorandum to Captain de Ste Croix which I will quote in full:

"*Bow and stern door remote indication*

Reference the Rec./Rep. submitted for the above and Mr. King's specification. I concur in part with Mr. King's penultimate paragraph that the project is unnecessary and not the real answer to the problem. In short, if the bow or stern doors are left open, then the person responsible for closing them should be disciplined. If it is still considered that some modification is required then a simple logic system, e.g. if the clam doors are open and the inner watertight doors closed then the door insecure alarm operates. The stern door on the other hand is visible from within the vehicle deck at all times, therefore the problem should not arise. So in conclusion, the Bridge indication is a 'no go'"

On the 28th October 1986 Captain de Ste Croix wrote a further memorandum to masters in which he said:

"Ron King has misjudged my requirements by submitting the attached specification. I consider that bridge indication is required for bow and stern W/T doors due to their extreme importance. He obviously thought I meant the outer bow doors because they cannot be seen when the inner bow doors are closed. Before I go back into print could I please have everyone's opinion? Do we all agree that it is required? To have bridge indication would be very expensive. Would indication on the mooring decks be sufficient? Ideas please."

18.8   Enough has been said to make it clear that by the autumn of 1986 the shore staff of the Company were well aware of the possibility that one of their ships would sail with her stern or bow doors open. They were also aware of a very sensible and simple device in the form of indicator lights which had been suggested by responsible Masters. That it was a sensible suggestion is now self-evident from the fact that the Company has installed indicator lights in their ships. That it was simple is illustrated by the fact that within a matter of days after the disaster indicator lights were installed in the remaining Spirit class ships and other ships of the fleet.

18.9   It seems probable that in respect of the 1986 suggestions no complaint would have been made if the fitting of indicator lights had been included in the specification for the next refit. In the event, the next refit for the *HERALD* was not due until after the casualty. It is only with the benefit of hindsight that it can now be seen that if in 1986 the matter had been treated with urgency it would probably have prevented this disaster. This topic has been discussed at length because it illustrates the attitude of the Marine Department to suggestions made by the Masters.

19. *Ascertaining draughts*

19.1 It is a legal requirement that the Master should know the draughts of his ship and that these be entered in the official log book before putting to sea. (See: Section 68(2) of the Merchant Shipping Act 1970 and the regulations made thereunder.) It was particularly important for the Master of the *HERALD* to know the draught of his ship because of the restriction in the number of passengers which the ship was entitled to carry if her draught exceeded 5.5 m moulded. It was even more important that the forward and aft draughts were read at Zeebrugge because of the necessity to trim the ship by the head in that port in order to load vehicles on to E deck.

19.2 Captain Lewry told the Court quite frankly that no attempt had been made to read the draughts of his ship on a regular basis or indeed at all in routine service. Fictitious figures were entered in the Official Log which took no account of the trimming water ballast. These figures, if they had been checked by anyone, would have indicated, incredibly, that the ship always sailed on an even keel. In fact the ship normally left Zeebrugge trimmed, and frequently trimmed by the head. Mr. Develin did not appreciate that the stability of the *HERALD* could be significantly affected if the ship was trimmed by the head. Mr. Develin is a Fellow of the Royal Institution of Naval Architects and has been a Government Marine Surveyor in Hong Kong. Accordingly he should have appreciated this. Whether the ship had sailed overloaded before the 6th March 1987 is not known, but seems likely.

19.3 The difficulties faced by the Masters are exemplified by the attitude of Mr. Develin to a memorandum dated 24th October 1983 and sent to him by Captain Martin.

The relevant passages of that memorandum are as follows:

> "For good order I feel I should acquaint you with some of the problems associated with one of the Spirit class ships operating to Zeebrugge using the single deck berths . . .
>
> 4. At full speed, or even reduced speed, bow wave is above belting forward, and comes three quarters of the way up the bow door . . .
>
> 6. Ship does not respond so well when trimmed so much by the head, and problems have been found when manoeuvring . . .
>
> 8. As you probably appreciate we never know how much cargo we are carrying, so that a situation could arise that not only are we overloaded by 400 tons but also trimmed by the head by 1.4 m. I have not been able to work out how that would affect our damage stability."

Mr. Develin was asked what he thought of that memorandum. His answer was: "Initially I was not happy. When I studied it further, I decided it was an operational difficulty report and Captain Martin was acquainting me of it." Later he said: "I think if he had been unhappy with the problem he would have come in and banged my desk." When Mr. Develin was asked what he thought about the information concerning the effect of full speed he said: "I believe he was exaggerating". In subsequent answers Mr. Develin made it clear that he thought every complaint was an exaggeration. In reply to a further question Mr. Develin said: "If he was that concerned he would not have sailed. I do not believe that there is anything wrong sailing with the vessel trimmed by the head." Mr. Develin ought to have been alert to the serious effects of operating at large trims. Furthermore he should have been concerned about Captain Martin's remarks about stability. He should at least have checked the ship's stability book. If he had done so he would have found that the ship was operating outside her conditions as set out and, therefore, not complying with the conditions under which the Passenger Ship Certificate was issued.

19.4 Mr. W. J. Ayers is a naval architect and he was at the relevant time a director of the Company. Mr. Ayers was a very unsatisfactory witness. He was verbose, rambling and at times misleading. In order to understand the difficulties which were experienced by the Masters it is necessary to look at some of the evidence in detail. On the 20th July 1982 Captain R. P. Blowers, the Senior Master of the *PRIDE* sent a most useful and helpful memorandum to Mr. Ayers in which Captain Blowers said:

> "With all our ships it is very difficult to read the draught with the result that for record purposes it is often as not guesstimated. Suggest fitting automatic draught recorders with read-out in the wheelhouse (I believe this system works on pressure)."

Mr. Ayers did not answer that memorandum.

19.5　Mr. Ayers told the Court that in his view it was impossible for the officers to read the draught marks of the *HERALD*. As that was his view it is, to say the least, surprising to find the following passage in a deposition sworn by Mr. Ayers in May 1987:

> "I have been aware of the difficulty of reading draught marks in cross-Channel ships since about 1948, and I have considered fitting remote-reading draught indication from time to time. In my view any equipment which goes on a cross-Channel ship must conform to the old-fashioned concept of fitness for purpose. With regard to draught, the benchmark of accuracy and legal standing is the draught marks and the load-line marks which are made in the presence of and to the satisfaction of the Department of Transport surveyor. By measurement of draught using these reference points, six in number, the mean draught and displacement can be accurately assessed, taking into account trim, heel, hog or sag. By comparison, equipment marketed to read draught is called an 'Indicator' and is no more than that. On a cross-Channel ferry it must be appreciated that one centimetre equals one average lorry and equipment which has an accuracy of plus or minus 10 centimetres cannot be used to determine whether ten lorries should be taken on or off the ship. It seems to me that if such equipment is to be used it must carry Department of Transport type approval and the accuracy be checked to the same standard as draught marks. In practice draught indictors within my limited experience have also had a totally unacceptable degree of reliability in the broader shipping scene."

19.6　It is now necessary to go back in time briefly. In 1982 the passenger ferry *EUROPEAN GATEWAY*, which was also owned by the Company, capsized after a collision off Harwich. Following that casualty the Company instituted an investigation into passenger safety. As a result of that investigation, on the 10th February 1983, Captain Martin sent a report to Mr. Develin. That report was seen by Mr. Ayers. It begins with the words:

> "The Company and ships' Masters could be considered negligent on the following points, particularly when some are the direct result of 'commercial interests'.
>
> (a) the ship's draught is not read before sailing, and the draught entered into the Official Log Book is completely erroneous; (Against this was written "Policy".)
>
> (b) It is not standard practice to inform the Master of his passenger figure before sailing.
>
> (The written comment was "system informs Master, who often does not agree the truth of the information. Working practice:")

27

(c) The tonnage of cargo is not declared to the Master before sailing.

(The comment against this was "working practice.")

(d) Full speed is maintained in dense fog.

(Against this the comment was "policy")."

The comments against each of those four items are very revealing. They were written by Mr. Michael Ayers, a member of the technical staff at Tonbridge. For the moment we are concerned only with draught reading. Later in that report under the heading "recommendations" there is the statement "company to investigate installing draught recorders on new tonnage." Mr. W. J. Ayers was asked whether he did investigate. His answer was "somewhere in this period the answer was yes". In the light of later answers given by Mr. W. J. Ayers, that answer is not accepted by the Court. It is necessary to quote verbatim some of the questions put to Mr. Ayers and his answers.

Q. You thought draught gauges were inaccurate?

A. Yes, sir.

Q. What tests did you carry out to see whether they were inaccurate?

A. Personally I have done none. It is just an industry reputation that I am working from.

Q. Have you ever used draught gauges yourself?

A. No, I have only had indirect news of draught gauges.

Q. Have you ever seen them used?

A. I have been on a ship, yes, but in studying the pamphlets the principal difficulty I have always faced is the analysis of fitness for service.

Q. I am just asking have you seen them used?

A. I have a feeling on a survey ship I have seen them.

Q. Do they give steady readings?

A. There is nothing to preclude it, yes. It must be so.

Q. In your investigation did you approach any manufacturers?

A. We have not seen a manufacturer in Tonbridge.

Q. Did you inspect any installations in your investigation?

A. No sir,

Q. Were you aware at that time of the different types available?

A. No.

Q. Would it be unfair of me to suggest that your investigation was pretty superficial?

A. With hindsight it can be said.

Mr. Ayers may be a competent Naval Architect, but the Court formed the view that he did not carry out his managerial duties, whatever they may have been. Mr. Ayers was asked whether each director of Townsend Car Ferries was given a specific area of responsibility. His answer was "No; there were not written guidelines for any director." When he was asked how each director knew what his responsibilities were his answer was "It was more a question of duplication as a result of not knowing than missing gaps. We were a team who had grown together." The amorphous phrasing of that answer is typical of much of the evidence of Mr. Ayers. He appeared to be incapable of expressing his thoughts with clarity.

28

19.7   Even this tragic disaster did not result in much immediate improvement. On the 7th May 1987 Mr. A. P. Young sent a memorandum to Mr. A. Black, who is a director of P. & O. in which he said:

> "Shore loading personnel expect ships' officers to advise if actual ship
> sinkage is ahead of estimated cargo tonnages. At this stage, the
> loading personnel will decide the shut-off priorities."

When Mr. Ayers was asked how the ships' officers could carry out that instruction his answer was "I do not believe they can possibly carry that out."

19.8   For the sake of completeness it is to be observed that at the time of the Investigation the deck log books provided to ships of this class did not contain any space for the entry of the draught on sailing. Steps have been taken to remedy that deficiency.

20. *The need for a high capacity ballast pump when trimming for the Zeebrugge berth.*

On the 28th February 1984 Mr. R.C. Crone, who was a Chief Engineer, sent a memorandum to Mr. Develin. The relevant parts are as follows:

Ballasting Spirit Class ships on Zeebrugge Service

Normal ballasting requirements are for Nos. 1 and 14 tanks . . . . to be filled for arrival Zeebrugge and emptied upon completion of loading . . . .

Using one pump the time to either fill or empty the two tanks is approximately 1hr. 55mins. Using two pumps on the common discharge the time can be reduced to approximately 1hr. 30mins . . . . .

Problems associated with the operation, ...

(a)   Pumping time amounts to approximately half the normal passage time.

(b)   Ship well down by the head for prolonged periods causing bad steerage and high fuel consumption.

(c)   Continuous pressurising of tanks to overflow/vent level.

(d)   Time consuming for staff.

(e)   Bow doors subjected to stress not normally to be expected, certainly having its effect on door locking gear equipment.

(f)   Dangerous complete blind operation that should not be carried out as normal service practice, i.e. no knowledge of tank capacity during operation, the tanks are pumped up until the overflow is noticed from the bridge, thereafter emptied until the pump amperage/pressure is noted to drop!

> Purely as a consideration realising the expense compared with possible future double ramp berths . . . . I would mention as follows:

> To fit to the Zeebrugge relief vessel one off approximate 1000cu met/hr 70KW pump. Unit with own sea chest and suctions together with suction and discharges to No. 14 tank and overboard, all to site in bow thrust compartment adjacent to tank.

Mr. Develin was asked about his reaction to that memorandum. He said that he did not agree with some of the contents. He appeared to think that the chief engineer was grossly exaggerating the problem. When Mr. Develin was asked what he did, he replied "Mr. Crone came on several occasions to the Marine Department and the matter went through as a technical project not connected with safety matters because the matter had been discussed with me." Mr. Develin appeared to think that the *HERALD* was designed to proceed at sea trimmed 1m by the head, despite the fact that he had no stability information for the ship in that trim. Mr. Develin said that Mr. Crone came to his department on several occasions to press for the implementation of his recommendations but that after discussion he must have been satisfied. Mr. Develin did not discuss Mr. Crone's memorandum with Mr. Parsons, or with Mr. Young or Mr. Ayers. Mr Develin was asked whether he thought the suggestion made by Mr. Crone that a powerful pump should be installed was a good idea or a bad idea. He said that he did not think he gave it much thought after having decided that it was not a safety matter. He handed it over as a technical project to Mr. Ridley. In due course an estimate was obtained for the installation of a pump at a cost of £25,000. This cost was regarded by the Company as prohibitive.

21. *Further management deficiencies*

21.1   Sufficient has been said to demonstrate that before the casualty those charged with the management of the Company's Ro-Ro fleet were not qualified to deal with many nautical matters and were unwilling to listen to their Masters, who were well qualified. Futhermore the shore management did not always support Masters who found it necessary to discipline members of their crew. In July 1985 Captain Kirby, the Senior Master of the *HERALD* lodged a protest that senior management had "advised" that penalties, which had been correctly imposed, should be rescinded because the crew threatened to strike. There had been a similar incident in the *PRIDE*. No Master can maintain discipline in his crew unless he has the confidence and backing of the management.

21.2   Mr. Barrett has recommended a new structure which will incorporate a Marine Operations Manager to whom the Masters of the various ships will report and who will himself report to the Fleet Director. Mr. Barrett recommends that the Marine Operations Manager should be a man with deck nautical experience.

22. *Was a statutory offence committed?*

22.1   Mr. Stone, who appeared on behalf of the Department, said, on instructions, that it is not the intention of the Department to prosecute anyone responsible for the fact that the *HERALD* went to sea with her bow doors open. There is implicit in that statement the suggestion that a statutory offence may have been committed. Mr. Steel who appeared on behalf of the Secretary of State, submitted that if a Ro-Ro ferry goes to sea with its bow doors open, that is not an offence under the Merchant Shipping Act 1979 or under the Merchant Shipping (Load Lines) Act 1967 or any other statute. Mr. Stone invited the Court to express its opinion as to whether that view is valid.

22.2   Neither the Master nor the Owners of the *HERALD* have been prosecuted. The offence which the Department has in mind has not been formulated. Accordingly neither the Master nor the Owners have been heard "in their own defence", save for some general submissions by Mr. Clarke on behalf of the Owners. Accordingly it would be quite unacceptable for this Court to express the view that a statutory offence was committed. The Court is able to deal with this question on this occasion because it is clearly of opinion that no statutory offence has been committed. There are however, four main reasons why it is undesirable that such a question should be raised before a Court of Formal Investigation in the future. (1) It is not the function of this Court to answer hypothetical questions. (2) It is not the function of this Court to express its opinion upon a question of construction of a statute, which does not arise in the course of the Investigation. (3) If this Court were to express its opinion upon the construction of a statute that view would not be binding upon a Magistrate's Court. (4) Finally, it might be inferred from a refusal by this Court to answer the question that a statutory offence had in fact been committed.

22.3   The relevant parts of section 44 of the Merchant Shipping Act 1979 are as follows;

44.   (1) If –
(a) A ship in a port in the United Kingdom; or

(b) A ship registered in the United Kingdom which is in any other port, is, having regard to the nature of the service for which the ship is intended, unfit by reason of the condition of the ship's hull, equipment or machinery, or by reason of undermanning or by reason of overloading or improper loading to go to sea without serious danger to human life, then, subject to the following subsection, the master and the owner of the ship shall each be guilty of an offence and liable on conviction on indictment to a fine and on summary conviction to a fine not exceeding £50,000.

(2) It shall be a defence in proceedings for an offence under the preceding subsection to prove that at the time of the alleged offence –

(a) arrangements had been made which were appropriate to ensure that before the ship went to sea it was made fit to do so without serious danger to human life by reason of the matters aforesaid which are specified in the charge; or

(b) it was reasonable not to have made such arrangements.

There is nothing in subsection 1 about "going to sea". The time at which an offence created by subsection 1 is committed must be when the ship is in port; the offence is that the ship is unfit to go to sea. No one would suggest that an offence was committed because the bow doors were open while the ship was being loaded. If it were to be alleged that an offence was committed between the completion of the loading and the moment of leaving the berth the defence of the Master and of the owners would have been that arrangements had been made which were appropriate to ensure that before the ship went to sea it was made fit to do so by closing the doors. This Court has no doubt that the words "the condition of the ship's hull, equipment or machinery" refer to that condition which would be reported upon by a surveyor and not to the *position* of doors, portholes, hatch covers and the like. If it is the view of Parliament that the taking to sea of a Ro-Ro ferry with her bow or stern doors open ought to be a criminal offence, then Parliament must enact appropriate legislation.

22.4   Mr. Stone submitted that an alternative Act under which the owner or master of the ship might have been prosecuted is the Merchant Shipping (Load Lines) Act 1967. The relevant parts of section 3 of that Act are as follows:

3. (1) Subject to any exemption conferred by or under this Act, no ship to which this Act applies, being a ship registered in the United Kingdom, shall proceed or attempt to proceed to sea unless –

(a) . . .

(b) . . .

(c) The ship complies with the conditions of assignment; and

(d) The information required by these rules to be provided as mentioned in subsection 2(4) of this Act is provided for the guidance of the master of the ship in the manner determined in accordance with the rules.

(2) If any ship proceeds or attempts to proceed to sea in
contravention of the preceding subsection, the owner or master
of the ship shall be guilty of an offence and liable on summary
conviction to a fine not exceeding £200.

This Act is concerned with the construction of the ship. The *HERALD* was in every respect properly constructed. The ship complied with the conditions of assignment. Mr. Stone was unable to spell out the offence which he submitted may have been committed. The Court has been unable to see any contravention of the provisions of that Act.

23. *The use of life-saving appliances*

23.1   The events of the night of 6th March when the *HERALD* capsized very rapidly precluded the deployment and use of any of the life-saving appliances except the lifejackets. The lifejackets were stowed principally in lockers adjacent to the Muster Stations on 'C' Deck, there being a locker port and starboard at each station. Those at frame 80 each contained about 280 jackets. There were nearly 500 jackets in each of the lockers at frame 25. The lockers were locked. The keys were in small glass crash boxes adjacent to the doors. When the ship capsized the doors on the starboard side would have opened downwards and those on the port side were submerged. All survivors reported masses of lifejackets floating in the water. It is not clear whether the doors on the starboard side burst open or were opened by persons unknown. The latter would have been extremely difficult as they were hanging over a void space. It seems unlikely that the jackets on the port side were released. They were probably forced out by their own buoyancy.

It is quite clear that the mass of floating jackets impeded some swimmers and prevented others from floating to the surface. Persons having access to lifejackets complained of difficulty in donning the jackets, untangling the tapes from other jackets and then discovering how to manipulate them. As hypothermia set in fingers became too numb to tie the tapes.

The standard lifejacket is intended to be donned under supervision in an orderly manner while waiting embarkation into lifeboats.

23.2   *Lifeboats*

Not one of the lifeboats was launched. Those on the starboard side were the source of much useful equipment which was used by the crew in the rescue operaton. This included the following:

Flares

Torches

Axes

Lifelines – Knotted ropes suspended from jackstays between the davits to assist the
boat's crew in lowering and boarding

Boarding ladders

Painters

Knives

24. *Rescue Operations*

24.1   There is set out in Appendix II an account of the search and rescue operations. There is set out in Appendix III a list of the ships which took part in those operations. The response of all the ships was immediate and without hesitation. All the ships rendered useful services.

The Court wishes to place on record and associate itself with the gratitude which was expressed by all parties in this Investigation for the outstanding services which were rendered by the Belgian people at all levels.

Belgian Air Force helicopters and Belgian Navy divers were also on the scene within a short time. They were the spearhead of an international rescue operation which included Royal Naval as well as Dutch and German naval personnel who were in the vicinity. They were directed from the Belgian Naval base.

The Court does not wish to be critical in any way of the very fine efforts which were made to rescue people from the capsized ship. But as a matter to which some thought may be given we would mention the need to be able to communicate with the helicopters. On this occasion their lights blinded the rescuers and rescued alike. Their noise made communication very difficult, if not impossible. The down-draught made it difficult to stand on the side of the ship.

On land the police, firemen and port emergency services were rapidly mobilised. Fleets of ambulances were ready to take survivors to six hospitals as soon as they were brought ashore. The hospitals were able to cope with the large influx of patients, some of whom were seriously injured. Red Cross volunteers from all walks of life rallied round to bring comfort to survivors and their relatives. The Governor of West Flanders, Mr. Olivier Vaneste, assumed control of the civilian operations soon after the accident. **In short, the response of the rescue services and of the Belgian people from the King and Queen and Prime Minister to the ordinary people living in and around Zeebrugge was magnificent.**

This brings to an end an account of the reasons for this very sad chapter in British maritime history. We now turn to consider ways in which life at sea in such ships may be made safer in the future.

PART II

The Future

25. *The purpose of the Investigation*

The statutory purpose of a Formal Investigation, which is held by virtue of an order made by the Department pursuant to section 55 of the Merchant Shipping Act 1970, is to inquire into the circumstances of the casualty and to establish its causes. But it has always been accepted that the Investigation has a second purpose, which is to see what lessons can be learned from the circumstances of the casualty which will contribute towards the safety of life at sea in the future. In this Investigation the second purpose has rightly assumed a major importance. It has occupied about one third of the hearing.

26. *The Policy of the Department*

Mr. Stone, speaking on behalf of the Department, said that it is important to establish a confidence that when a Court of Formal Investigation makes recommendations they are looked at closely, studied in consultation with others and acted upon. The Court has that confidence and expresses the hope that readers of this Report will appreciate that the Department takes serious note of all comments made in such a report. The Court sees the good sense in the policy that after studying suggestions and recommendations some will not be implemented until there is international agreement. Mr. Stone summarised the advantages of such a policy in two main points: First, it has the advantage that there will be cross-fertilisation of ideas which contribute to a world-wide advance in standards of safety at sea, and second, it is likely to produce agreement upon an international standard which can be incorporated in an identifiable system of certification.

27. *Degrees of urgency*

27.1   There are, however, some recommended safety measures, which are comparatively inexpensive, and which appear to be so eminently desirable that this country should take unilateral action by Regulations affecting ships flying the British flag after proper consultation with such persons in the United Kingdom as the Secretary of State considers will be affected by those measures.

27.2   Some of the evidence gave rise to concern about a number of current practices, both in terms of technical procedures and in relation to basic design and approval. There was some evidence of a need for changes in the basic design of Ro/Ro passenger ferries. It is not the function of this Court to attempt to re-design the entire ferry fleet. But the evidence has led the Court to conclude that there are some areas in which action is called for immediately, others in which action should be taken in the near future and yet others in which serious consideration should be given to changes in design in the longer term. We will deal with each of the categories in turn. The matters which call for immediate attention fall into three broad categories. (A) Those relating to the safety of the ship, (B) those relating to loading and the stability of the ship and (C) those relating to the saving of life in an emergency.

Immediate action

    (A) Safety of the ship

28. *Indicator lights*

The Court heard much evidence regarding bridge indicator lights and the need for them. Their fitting is now required by the Department, but there are aspects of such lights which need clarification. Evidence was heard as to alleged unreliability of indicator lights, particularly in relation to the microswitches used for actuating the circuits. This evidence from Townsend Thoresen mainly concerned microswitches with exposed moving mechanical parts e.g. pivoted arms. The Court considers that the preferred form should be a proximity switch, e.g. a totally enclosed watertight reed type, such as is used commonly in ships.

The lights should not only indicate in a suitable position on the bridge, but the entire circuit should be designed on a fail-safe basis so that if there should be an electrical failure in any switch circuit the system would indicate danger.

Indicator lights should be fitted to all superstructure doors, such as passenger access, bunkering and storing doors.

It is desirable that a dedicated door alarm panel be fitted, similar to that commonly used for watertight doors.

Finally, the condition of superstructure door indicator lights should be logged before departure just as is the condition of the watertight doors below the bulkhead deck.

29. *Closed circuit television*

For some years a number of Baltic ferries and certain other ferries outside the United Kingdom have used closed circuit television sureveillance of the cargo spaces, the superstructure shell doors and the engine room.

The purpose has been to:-

    (a)   monitor the condition of the doors and convey that information to the bridge.

    (b)   check the vehicle decks for intruders, whether innocent or otherwise and to check whether there is any movement of vehicles in a seaway.

    (c)   keep the bridge aware of conditions in the engine room.

Freight vehicles should always be secured. If they are unsecured even a tight turn may shift them, with a dramatic effect on stability. Closed circuit television can give warning of such movement. Also it must be recognised that the vehicle deck of a ferry is of potential interest to thieves and terrorists. During a passage the vehicle decks are out-of-bounds, except to the crew. **Closed circuit television surveillance is a valuable addition to safety precautions. For this reason we consider it to be a feature that should be recommended to ferry operators.**

However the most important use of closed circuit television in the vehicle decks is to monitor the condition of bow doors, both inner and outer, stern doors and any side doors. While the system must depend primarily upon proper procedures for closing, then reporting and logging, and indicator lights are a valuable additional source of information for the bridge, closed circuit television is helpful in that it enables the Master to see his personnel shutting the doors. This is especially so if a remote control zoom lens is used which can pick up the dogs and latches. **We have no doubt that closed circuit television monitoring of all superstructure doors, is well worthwhile and should be fitted.**

30. *Berth alterations*

It has been found that ships such as the *HERALD* can shut their bow or stern doors at some berths before leaving. At others ships cannot close their doors until the ramp has been raised. It is not only desirable but imperative that doors should be shut before leaving the berth. It follows that if ships cannot shut their doors at a particular berth, because of the design of that berth, then alterations should be made to the berth.

Alterations have been made to some berths, but it is considered by the Court that all berths on U.K. routes should be altered so that ships with clam shell doors or normal stern doors are able to shut their doors before leaving the berth. It is more difficult for ships with visor bows, which must pull back somewhat from the ramp before they can close the visor. But the fact that the visor bow is open is obvious to the Master. Indeed the ship cannot be navigated until the bow visor has been lowered. This is, therefore, not a serious problem provided the inner door is shut before leaving the berth. **It is desirable that each berth should then carry an approval certificate specifically listing the ships which can operate from it, and can shut their bow and stern doors without moving from the berth.** Parliament may wish to consider whether it should be an offence for a ferry to leave a berth before its bow and stern doors are closed.

(B) Loading and stability

31. *Draught gauges*

We have already mentioned the difficulty, if not impossibility, of reading the aft draught on many ferries, which is due to the extreme flare of the ship's sides as a result of the wide sterns of such ships. The evidence of Mr. Ayers and others drew attention to this difficulty. Several members of the Court have extensive experience of using draught gauges, and reference was made at the hearing to the ample information available from manufacturers which the Court has seen.

Draught gauges or indicators are of several types, for example pneumatic and electrical. They are available from a number of manufacturers in different countries and have been in use for many years. **The Court concludes that mechanical, pneumatic, electrical or hydrostatic draught gauges or indicators should be a requirement for Ro/Ro passenger ferries, using types specifically investigated and approved by the Department.** These gauges or indicators should be fitted to give readout at the aft and forward loading positions and on the bridge. Desirably they should indicate the aft and forward draughts and the midships draught. The latter should not be a mean of the fore and aft draughts but should be a mean of sensors, port and starboard, giving a true draught at the loadline mark.

Draught gauges or indicators should, if possible, be suitable for interfacing with a loadicator so that if weight information for vehicles is fed into the loadicator a running automatic up-date of the ship's condition could be produced. **It is recommended that the loadicator be in a suitable central position with, if possible, work stations at the two loading stations and on the bridge.**

32. *Freight weights*

The question of automated weigh bridges and loadicators is considered elsewhere. In the absence of immediate information being available from weigh bridges it is recognised that for some time the weight of cargo of Ro-Ro ferries will be predicted on the basis of declared weights for freight and of nominal weights for smaller vehicles such as cars and coaches. A reliable procedure is necessary.

The practice of using one metric tonne for the all-up weight of the average car with luggage, fuel, and personal effects, is outmoded. A nominal weight of $1\frac{1}{4}$ metric tonnes should be adopted. This figure should be reviewed regularly by the Department on a large random sample basis, say, every five years.

Similar considerations apply to coaches, where the current Townsend Thoresen practice of allowing 14 tons per coach should be adopted. **It is desirable that the Department should conduct an analysis of coaches, particularly of the long distance double decker type, in order to determine a more accurate basis for the nominal weight.** This nominal weight should then be used in making up the cargo predictions.

Finally, there is the very important question of freight vehicle weights. Partly because the permissible weight limits on the Continent are higher than in the United Kingdom there is an advantage to be gained in under-declaring the weight of freight vehicles proceeding from the Continent to the United Kingdom. It is not enough to say that this will only apply to vehicles coming into the United Kingdom because if a vehicle is leaving the United Kingdom for a long Continental run, there is also an advantage for the British operator to load to the Continental limit.

Checks at Dover on over 100 vehicles coming to the United Kingdom showed that on average the actual weight exceeded the declared weight by approximately 13%. It is considered that these checks should be extended, particularly covering the present gap in knowledge of the weight of outgoing vehicles.

The checks should not be on the basis of weighing obviously likely vehicles, but on a purely random basis. To avoid criticism of the statistical validity of such checks, a considerable number of vehicles should be covered, say 500 either way. Such numbers, in conjunction with a random choice, should produce a reliable margin for addition to the waybill declaration. Meanwhile we consider that an addition of 13% should be made to declared weights when making up anticipated cargoes.

This does not, however, replace the necessity to read draughts accurately to prevent overloading, nor does it replace the need for weigh bridges and individual weight measurements for every heavy vehicle loading onto a Ro-Ro ferry. Its main value, in the context of accurately read draughts, is to allow reliable determination of the ratio of weight being loaded on the upper and lower decks of a two-tier ferry. This ratio can be crucial, as was shown by evidence of Mr. Taggart.

Finally, once a comprehensive weigh bridge system is instituted the Department should review the statistics of declared and actual weights and produce an update of such margins every five years.

33. *Weigh bridge certificates*

In view of the uncertainty as to the actual weights of many freight vehicles every effort should be made to persuade, or even require, Port Authorities to provide rolling weigh-bridges, possibly of the loadcell type, where all freight vehicles coming into a port will be automatically weighed and issued with a weight certificate, to be attached to the vehicle.

If such weigh bridges were fitted in way of each ramp it would be possible to pass this information electronically to the loadicator, thus updating the calculated condition of the ship if the loading officer punched in vehicle locations. **The Court concludes that the Department should encourage Operators to investigate immediately the technical and practical aspects of the proposal.** As the calculation of fluid KG (or GM) of a Ro-Ro vessel prior to departure should be obligatory such a system would be of real assistance in carrying this out.

(C) Live Saving

34. *The problems on this occasion*

The evidence of surviving passengers and crew has brought to light what may have appeared to them to have been deficiencies in the appliances available for helping them to survive this disaster. In the light of what occurred and of the comments and complaints made by survivors, fresh thought can, and no doubt will, be given to the question: what life saving appliances ought to be provided? The Court wishes to make it clear that, in drawing attention to matters which have been mentioned, it does so without the slightest criticism. The *HERALD* was well supplied with life-saving appliances. No two catastrophes occur in the same way or give rise to the need for the same equipment. However much thought is devoted to considering what equipment is most likely to be useful on the next occasion, no one can foretell what the circumstances will be. The main problems which faced those who survived this disaster were:

    1. The lack of illumination

    2. The difficulty in donning lifejackets.

    3. The lack of apertures through which to escape.

    4. The difficulty of climbing up to such apertures as there were.

35. *Emergency Lighting*

A distressing feature of the *HERALD* accident was the lack of emergency lighting. While the emergency lighting came on during the capsize, it went off again almost immediately. This is not surprising as it was on a circuit of which parts were immersed when the ship went on her beam ends. In any event emergency generators are incapable of operating at large angles of heel.

The Court heard evidence from survivors and members of the ship's crew that underlined the grave effect that this absence of light had upon both morale and the practicality of rescue. It also heard evidence from Mr. Graham, a Principal Engineering Surveyor with the Department, as to the engineering aspects of the problem and the equipment available for its solution.

Mr. Graham described several types of available self-contained emergency lighting and came to the conclusion that the so called 'self-contained maintained light' was the best system to use. We agree. This type of unit generally uses Ni-cad batteries and is on continuous charge. Normally a bulb is illuminated the whole time. It may be arranged so that it lights only when the charge is broken. If it is alight the whole time, the advantage is that it can be seen to be working.

As a matter of urgency, self-contained, maintained emergency lighting units of a type approved by the Department should be fitted to all Ro/Ro passenger ferries in suitable numbers and in such places as may be advised by the Department. It is essential in our view that such units should be watertight – in other words, if the unit should be submerged it should remain alight until the batteries run down.

Furthermore, a regular routine check on the condition of this emergency lighting should be a requirement. This could perhaps be a weekly inspection by the ship's electrical officer followed by logging that all was in order.

36. *Lifejackets*

We have already drawn attention to the difficulties experienced in donning lifejackets. We include the topic in this part of the Report merely as a reminder that it is a matter to which consideration should now be given.

37. *Toughened Glass*

During the rescue operations a considerable number of people were saved by being lifted, or by climbing up ladders and ropes, through starboard side windows which had been broken by rescuers.

These windows were made of heat treated toughened glass which does not break into large shards as does plate glass or remain cracked but unbroken as does laminated safety glass. Instead it crumbles into small particles which are not dangerous and which can be knocked out of the apertures.

This type of toughened glass tends to break and drop out when exposed to flame. Laminated safety glass on the other hand will last much longer and it is for this reason that Mr. Taggart, Principal Surveyor in the Marine Directorate, informed the Court that the Department was asking for laminated glass in way of lifeboat embarkation stations in order to improve fire safety.

In the light of the *HERALD* rescue operations this was a disturbing answer. Mr. Taggart was examined by the Court on this point:–

Q. You have talked about glass windows and partitions. I was interested and relieved to hear you talk about toughened glass and grain size. If the side windows of the *HERALD* had been made of laminated safety glass on the one hand, or polycarbonate on the other, what would have been the situation on the night of the tragedy?

A. I suspect that the majority of people would have been lost.

Q. In other words, there is a very good reason to specify toughened glass in such a situation rather than anything else?

A. Oh yes, we have not . . . unfortunately you have got, conflicting requirements. Fire is a very significant hazard. To stick to toughened glass without the laminate would probably on a risk basis, be worse than . . . you know I think the risk of fire is greater in this respect and the risk of fire to the life saving deployment.

Q. In the last 50 years how many passengers on ferries have lost their lives through fire, if any?

A. None but there have been fires and if we can solve the problem in some other way I would not feel we should be talking to reducing a potential safety factor, i.e. the fire resistant glass; it would be far preferable to find another means of solving our problem.

Mr. Taggart went on to talk about his preference for preventing capsizes and also about escape windows, but this exchange underlines a serious position where, on the one hand, the Department is asking for laminated glass in way of lifeboat stations in the deckhouses and, on the other hand, have behind them the dreadful experience of the *HERALD* where, if it had not been for the use of toughened rather than laminated glass, in their opinion the majority of the people on board would have been lost.

We consider this to be an issue that must be tackled with vigour and urgency. If laminated safety glass is to be used in windows in way of lifeboat and embarkation stations, it is clear that they should, if possible, be fitted in push-out or centre line hinged window frames in situations where rapid exit through the windows may be necessary. In other areas it is essential to stay with heat treated toughened glass, with the minimum grain size compatible with the other desired characteristics.

In this respect there is clearly a need for a good standardised industry approach to escape windows. These should be reliable and uncomplicated and openable from either side.

38. *Means of Escape*

Many modern Ro-Ro passenger ferries are arranged on a semi open plan layout of passenger compartments with no side exit at all for a considerable length fore and aft.

Access and exit on the same level is generally from the ends of such spaces and from an amidships set of doors. There is vertical access from and through these spaces.

The Court thinks that in general, the design of slab sided vessels should be discouraged. The main objections to them are:–

1. They eliminate outboard fore and aft escape routes.

2. Embarkation stations often have to be on the top deck, which is very high above the water.

It is in the context of current design that the importance of being able to break side windows arises, not only if a ship is on her beam ends, but also to allow the possibility of escape in extreme circumstances when the ship is upright. Athwartships doors should be provided at recognised intervals; and thought should be given to providing access to them with the ship at significant angles of heel, say in excess of 20°. Additionally, it is a matter of some concern that passengers should be able to recognise readily escape routes and doors allowing exit athwartships from these long passenger compartments. Prominent labelling of decks, exits, lifejacket stows and muster stations is important. The Court considers that designers and the Department should give attention to these matters.

Another matter of concern is the efficiency of emergency exits from accommodation below bulkhead deck. A steward, Mr. Butler, heard water running down the stairs from G deck to the lower accommodation. This must have been going over the sill from the vehicle deck which was 200 mm in height. Consideration should be given to whether such sills should be higher, say 600 mm. The *HERALD* had two main passenger compartments below the bulkhead deck, between frames 105–118 and between 118–132. Each of these was fitted with two means of escape in accordance with the P.S.C. Regulations 1980. However, there was a watertight door between the two passenger compartments and this was often kept open for convenience and access. If this door was open during the casualty that was not causative. Nevertheless such a door should be kept shut at sea and not used as an escape route. This is a matter which should be implemented immediately.

Furthermore, there should be immediately a general safety audit of means of escape from passenger compartments below bulkhead decks in existing ships to ensure that:–
(a) they comply with the relevant Passenger Ship Regulations, and
(b) that the Regulations themselves are being applied properly and rigorously.

A single means of escape from spaces below the bulkhead deck is dangerous. Supplementary escapes should take into account the possibility that collision damage or submergence may render them useless.

39. *Movement facility in a ship on her beam ends.*

The *EUROPEAN GATEWAY* and the *HERALD* ended up on their beam ends in shallow water.

We have already mentioned that in the *HERALD* considerable difficulty was caused by transverse alleyways which became deep vertical shafts when the ship was at 90°. While suggestions have been made as to the desirability of finding some means of bridging these shafts, it is the view of the Department of Transport that this is not really practicable. the Court is not convinced by this. It considers that simple methods of bridging should be developed. For example, split deckhead panels hinged in way of the sides of a longitudinal passage could be arranged so that with the ship on her beam ends one of these panels could be brought down and made to bridge the gap. It would be self-supporting if it extended fore and aft beyond the sides of the transverse alley way. There may well be **better methods, but some such simple device should be developed and made a requirement.**

40. *Additional items*

In addition to the matters already mentioned there was substantial agreement between the parties that consideration should be given to the following matters:

1. Whether lockers should be fitted on the upper deck on each side of Ro-Ro ferries. Those lockers should contain equipment such as axes, torches, ladders, ropes, lifting devices and harnesses (including some for small children)

2. Whether glass partitions should be designed with intermittent gaps.

3. Apart from those mentioned in 1 above, whether a supply of harnesses for adults and children would be useful, Consideration should be given to including them in standard lifeboat equipment. Many survivors were too numb, weak or lacking in skill to secure a rope around themselves or others.

4. Whether there could be permanent footholds in alleyways to assist movement at extreme angles of heel.

Action in the near future

41. *Definitions*

"Bulkhead deck" means the uppermost deck up to which transverse watertight bulkheads are carried.

The "margin line" is an imaginary line 76 mm below the bulkhead deck at the side of the ship and following it throughout the length of the ship.

A "one compartment ship" is a ship which is so constructed as to provide sufficient intact stability in all service conditions to enable the ship to withstand the flooding of any one of her main compartments.

A "two compartment ship" has sufficient intact stability to withstand the flooding of two adjacent compartments.

"One compartment condition" and "two compartment condition" have corresponding meanings.

"I.M.O." (the International Maritime Organization) includes, where the context so requires, its predecessor I.M.C.O. (the Intergovernmental Maritime Consultative Organization)

"PSC" means Passenger Ship Construction.

"PSC & S" means Passenger Ship Construction and Survey.

Note: There are "Rules" up to 1965 and "Regulations" thereafter.

42. *Provision of stability information and limiting KG envelope curves*

The *HERALD* was constructed substantially under the Merchant Shipping (PSC) Regulations 1980. These Regulations were paralleled by the Regulations on Sub-division and Stability of Passenger Ships 1974, published by I.M.O. The Court heard evidence on a number of aspects of stability under the 1980 Regulations with which we will deal.

The Stability Booklet of the *HERALD* was in accordance with Schedule 2 and Regulation 9 of the 1980 Regulations. This required, inter alia, diagrams and a statement for each of a number of conditions, including the loading condition on departure and arrival when loaded to the deepest sub-division lines, (both C1 and C2) and loading condition for service loads. A worst anticipated service condition was required, on which the damage stability requirements of regulation II and Schedule 3 of the 1980 Regulations were based and in addition a graph or table of maximum allowable vertical centre of gravity (KG).

Where there was a significant amount of trim in any of these conditions the metacentric height and the curve of righting levers were to be determined from the trimmed water line as required by sub-paragraph (4) of paragraph 10 of Schedule 2.

In the Stability Book of the *HERALD* a curve of limiting fluid vertical centre of gravity (KG_f) against draught was provided for each of the one and two compartment conditions.

The purpose of the limiting KG_f curve is to provide easily usable information for the Master and Officers so that they can determine whether any given loading condition falls within the operating limits of the vessel. Clearly this requires the calculation of KG_f and the accurate reading of draughts. In service neither of these requirements were met by those operating the *HERALD* throughout her career, but, nevertheless, the information was available to be used.

The limiting KG_f curves for the C1 and C2 conditions were drawn for level keel. Furthermore the hydrostatic information in the Stability Book and the cross curves of stability were computed also for level keel.

However, a number of the conditions in the Book were at an appreciable trim. For example, the C2 mark departure condition at 0.23 m trim, the corresponding condition with 50% consumption at 0.35 m trim and the corresponding arrival condition at 0.53 m trim. These are 'two compartment' conditions and definitive.

In the two compartment arrival condition with only E deck loaded the trim was 0.89 m by the stern and in the corresponding one compartment condition 0.93 m by the stern. Thus the operating spectrum for the *HERALD* encompassed substantial trims. Furthermore, the relief service to Zeebrugge, which the *SPIRIT* Class vessels carried out, frequently required substantial trims by the head at the berth. These trims have never been quantified accurately but appear to have exceeded 1 m on occasion.

The approval by the Department of the Stability Book with such trimmed conditions and, indeed, with others up to about 0.9 m, all based on level keel hydrostatics and GZ curves, does not appear to conform with paragraph 10 (4) of schedule 2.

Limiting KG_f curves were computed for the Court by the sub-division section of the Department and were submitted in evidence. these were calculated for level keel and trims of ½ m and 1 m by the stern and by the bow. It was found that for one compartment damage the Department curves, with 50 mm residual GZ as the main criterion, for all conditions gave significantly higher value of permissible KG_f than the builders' one compartment standard curve. With 100 mm residual GZ the curves were at a level similar to that of the builders. All one compartment conditions in the Stability Book were below the Department's permissible curves and met the trimmed limits.

In the two compartment condition the situation was different. Residual GZ was the dominant criterion at draughts up to about 5.2 m. Above that draught and up to the extreme limiting draught of 5.52 m, margin line immersion became dominant. Up to approximately 5.3 m for all trims by the stern and by the head the permissible KG_fs were higher than the limiting line in the Stability Book. Above 5.3 m margin line immersion rapidly became critical.

At level keel the Department line was well above the Builders' limiting line. With the presence of initial trim, however, the picture was quite different. With ½ m trim by the stern the Department's result was lower than the builders' line at draughts exceeding 5.35 m. At 5.52 m (the C2 extreme draught) the limiting KG_f was only 9.65 m as against the Builders' figure of 10.2 for level keel.

With 1 m trim by the stern the department's KG_f limit fell below that of the Builders at 5.25 m, and at the C2 mark was 7.66 m as against 10.2 m.

With trim by the head the results were similar but worse. Again at ½ m trim by the head the Department's results were dominated by GZ criteria up to a draught of 5.2 m, but thereafter margin line immersion became dominant, the Department's line dropping below that of the Builders at 5.3 m draught. At the C2 mark draught and at 1 m trim the maximum permissible KG was 2.39 m against the Builders' figure of 10.2 m.

The Court was most concerned by these serious, but not unexpected, results. The calculations were checked by the Department, which was questioned as to their reliability. The Department confirmed that the calculations could be relied upon.

Mr. Taggart was asked the following questions:-

Q.   At that time did the Department realise that the permissible KG curve was quite strongly affected by trim, "at that time" meaning at the time of the approval of the Stability Book? (For the *HERALD*).

A.   I cannot make a positive statement, of course, because I was not involved. I think it is probable that they did not anticipate it being so severely affected as seems to have been demonstrated.

Q. The curve does appear to be quite strongly affected by the trim does it not?

A. Yes.

Q. Why not simply require that instead of the unique permissible KG curve, you have the level keel one plus something like, shall we say, 4% trim by the head and 8% trim by the head and similarly by the stern? This would give the Master information which would cover any conceivable operating condition would it not?

A. Yes that is true.

Further:

Q. If it can produce everything for a particular trim at a particular draught in a matter of three or four hours, (computertime) is that a very onerous burden when talking of a ship costing perhaps £30M?

A. No. I admit it would certainly cover the entire possibilities then. Perhaps we should adopt this practice and require this more comprehensive analysis of ships in the future. I was only describing the philosophy of the Department up to the present.

Q. You see what I am getting at really is to try to find out from you whether there is a procedure that avoids judgement as to the susceptibility of a particular hull form for margin line immersion — with a particular condition which requires an individual calculation. These curves would be all embracing, would they not?

A. Yes.

The question of deballasting at sea was also covered in Mr. Taggart's evidence. He pointed out that the 1984 Regulations would require calculation of both the original departure condition and a near final condition, the latter having low added weight but large free surface. The 1984 Regulations do not, however, require any damage stability calculations to be carried out to determine whether the ship might become unsafe, if breached, during the operation. Mr. Taggart was asked about this as follows;-

Q. If you had, during the deballasting, a particular trim, shall we say, and you had a lot of free surface you could, especially if you had an onboard computer, run out a KG_f and check it on the trim curves?

A. Yes that would be immensely useful to the Master in that respect.

The Master has responsibility for operating the vessel inside the permissible limits of the Stability Book. Information is provided to enable him to do this, but a Stability Book such as that of the *HERALD* does not permit him to carry out meaningful calculations to determine whether the ship meets the requirements when trimmed significantly. Obviously the Master cannot carry out damage stability calculations. Thus he has no guide at all as to the safety of the ship at a substantial trim.

For the *HERALD* with a trim by the stern the load departure condition at the C2 mark and its corresponding arrival condition would both be at vertical centres of gravity higher than the values which would permit the ship to retain two compartment standard. In other words, on any voyage which the *HERALD* or her sisters made (or makes) near the C2 mark with a trim of ¼–½ m by the stern the vessel may be in a one compartment condition and not two, as required by the C2 mark.

This is disturbing. If there is a large passenger load it is potentially dangerous. It is now apparent that the Department and IMO may not have recognised fully the importance of initial trim upon damaged stability, flooding and margin line immersion.

The concept of a curve of maximum allowable vertical centre of gravity versus draught was introduced in the Regulations on Sub-Division and Stability of Passenger Ships produced by IMO in 1974 (Regulation 8 (b)(i)). This however does not recognise any potential effect of initial trim and requires a simple, unique, curve.

In the PSC Regulations 1980 (Schedule 2 paragraph 12) there is a requirement for a curve or table of required metacentric height (GM) versus draught, or alternatively of maximum allowable vertical centre of gravity (KG) versus draught. These are based upon compliance with the intact stability requirements of Regulation 10 and the damage stability requirements of Regulation 11 and Schedule 3

43

of those Regulations. This is set out at paragraph 10 (2) of Schedule 2, and is repeated in the 1984 Regulations.

In the latter, a worst anticipated service condition is still required and there is, rightly, a new requirement that cross-curves should be determined taking into account the change in trim due to heel. (See paragraph 9 (1) of Schedule 2.)

It is remarkable, however, that even in the 1984 Regulations the requirement regarding minimum allowable metacentric height or maximum allowable vertical centre of gravity is for a single curve, and, while not specifically mentioned, it is implicit that this is for level keel.

Thus even in the 1984 British Regulations there is no recognition of the importance of initial trim upon damaged stability, flooding and margin line submersion. This is strange because the reason for the effect is simple. As Mr. Taggart said "the limiting criterion is usually on the non-immersion of the margin line. When you have an initial trim, the freeboard is reduced even before you start flooding the damaged compartment.'

The Court's unease was increased when Mr. Taggart was asked about the two new ships, *PRIDE OF DOVER* and *PRIDE OF CALAIS*:-

Q   What has been asked for on the *PRIDE OF DOVER* and the *PRIDE OF CALAIS*? Is the maximum KG fluid curve going to cover trims?

A.   We have gone to the builders and drawn their attention to the fact that their calculations are currently based on level trim and that they would be required to augment the information if they intend to depart from that.

Q.   So that until you drew their attention to this point, they were producing level keel information?

A.   Yes.

The Department of Transport wrote to Schichau Unterweser A.G. on the 19th February 1987 following completion of their check of the damage stability for the vessel. In this letter there is no apparent appreciation of the effect of initial trim upon the KG_f envelope curve against draught. It is difficult to reconcile Mr. Taggart's replies with the contents of that letter, leading the Court to conclude that prior to the casualty the Department did not appreciate the impact of initial trim upon the limiting KG_f curve. A copy of the letter of 19th February was produced by the Department only after the conclusion of the speeches. This was unfortunate as it did not give Mr. Taggart an opportunity to explain answers which appear to be misleading.

Suitable curves have now been issued to the remaining *SPIRIT* class vessels showing KG_f envelopes for level keel and trims of 300 mm and 500 mm by bow and stern. There is also an embargo upon trims exceeding 500 mm. This latter limit may be over-generous in the light of some of the two compartment conditions in the original Stability Book. These curves are of a satisfactory type provided guidance be given to the Masters for interpolation for other trims.

There should be a requirement in the PSC & S Regulations for standard KG_f envelope curves, at least for level keel and trims by the stern and by the head of, say, 0.4% and 0.8% of the length of the ship.

In view of the importance of this point, the Court considers that requirements should be imposed upon all existing ferries for the provision of such initial trim curves. These should be implemented within a short time to prevent operation at unsuitable (and possibly dangerous) trims and vertical centres of gravity.

The Court also considers that all existing Stability Books for Ro-Ro passenger ferries should be reviewed in detail by the department. Furthermore, during the review of existing books they should be examined to see whether they provide adequate information for the assessment of safe loading in respect of factors such as the tabulation of vertical centres of gravity for cargo on all vehicle decks. A standardised vertical centre of gravity should be used for each type of vehicle.

Clearly the vertical height of the centre of gravity (KG) of the vessel itself is of importance. In view of the considerable weight increases apparent in the *SPIRIT* and *PRIDE* **it is likely that not only the weight but also the vertical and longitudinal centres of gravity of the lightship have altered significantly for all or most of the Ro-Ro passenger ferries in service.** This should be taken into account when preparing the curves.

43. *Growth of lightship*

Lightship checks on the *SPIRIT* and *PRIDE* indicated increases in their lightship weights averaging 263 tonnes of which some 116 were on account of many known modifications. The latter were all of a minor nature, none individually justifying a major re-assessment of lightship.

The increase over and above the known modifications amounts to approximately 0.3% per annum – a high figure. There are many ferries in service older than the *SPIRIT* class. With them all there are likely to be substantial increases in their lightship weight. Such increases may have occurred at considerable heights above the keel, particularly in respect of paint, catering stores, seating, and the like.

In view of the importance of the KG_f envelope upon damage trim stability an up to date knowledge of the weight of lightship and its vertical centre of gravity is essential for all existing ferries. Not only should the *SPIRIT* class vessels be re-inclined, but **all existing ferries that have not been re-inclined within the last 4 years should be re-inclined as a matter of urgency to assess their current lightship weights and centres of gravity.** Thereafter they should be re-inclined at every special survey. These figures would then be available for use in the production of reliable trimmed KG_f envelope curves.

44. *Responsibility for stability during unloading and loading.*

While at sea a Ro-Ro ferry, like any other ship, is operated in accordance with the requirements of the Stability Book. In port the ship may be loaded in such a way that there may be high transient cargo centres of gravity, or the ship may be trimmed to allow access to bow or stern doors, or may heel substantially during the movement of particularly heavy units of freight. In these respects Ro-Ro ferries differ from other ships handling cargo.

Evidence was put before the Court showing that several serious accidents have occurred in port during unloading/loading.

If extreme trims are to be used during unloading or loading, the Stability Book should contain sufficient information to enable a Master to assess the safety of a particular operation, even though that information may not be relevant to seagoing conditions

On Day 26 Mr. Taggart was asked:–

Q. Whose writ runs following a Ro-Ro ship arriving at a berth, that is, let us say, between a loaded arrival condition and starting to unload – later reaching a loaded departure condition. During the actual unloading and loading operation does a Stability Booklet still hold?

A. No.

Q. It does not?

A. No.

Q. Does the Ministry, the Department of Transport, have jurisdiction over the ship during that time?

A. Not as far as I am aware, no.

Q. Who does in a British or foreign port?

A. It is possible that the Health Safety Executive might have some input while she is in port.

Q. Is the ship out on her own during that period, or is it the Port Authority who is in charge of her?

A. I am afraid I can only, without investigation, speak to the Department's responsibility and that would not run in that situation.

Q. If it is the Port Authority, do some ships go to ports where, to all intents and purposes, there are no Port Authorities?

A. Yes.

Q. So the ship is at that time on her own?

A. Yes it is obvious from a loading point of view. It is up to the Master to be prudent in his loading procedures.

Q. There have been accidents to Ro-Ro ships which have trimmed themselves heavily by the head in port?

A. Yes this can be addressed from a design point of view . . . etc.

The Court is concerned by this situation because, if the Master is to be held responsible for the unloading and loading in port, he must be provided with all the information needed to make a responsible assessment. At present the Department does not require the Stability Book to provide such information.

It is appreciated that hydrostatic data for large trims, especially by the head are not relevant to sea going conditions. However, they may be necessary for loading and unloading. For example those on board the *HERALD* and her sister ships working out of Zeebrugge on spring high tides could not have known how stable their ships were in a static sense. In fact they were stable; the class being relatively insensitive in this respect to head trims. But other ships with wide, flat, lightly immersed sterns could experience large reductions in metacentric height when trimmed by the head.

The Department should state that trims should never exceed certain limits, or alternatively and preferably, **hydrostatic data for large trims should be included in the Stability Booklet, but noted as being for harbour guidance only.** Furthermore, the Stability Book should emphasise the need to keep a running check upon metacentric height at the relevant trims during the unloading/loading operations. **The Stability Book or Approved Program must apply to all operating conditions, not only to seagoing conditions.**

Longer term recommendations
45. *Design*

In essence ferries are powered pontoons on top of which vehicles are carried. The vehicle space is enclosed by a superstructure not only to protect the vehicles, but also to give an adequate range of stability and to support accommodation.

The superstructure must have doors to allow access for the vehicles and these are usually, but not always, at the ends. Obviously the doors have to be weathertight when closed, to ensure the buoyancy of the superstructure.

The conventional Ro-Ro passenger ferry carries a mix of freight vehicles, cars and other vehicles on one or more decks running the whole length of the ship. A few ferries are designed to carry trains on the bulkhead deck. The economic viability of such vessels depends strongly upon the carriage of large, freight vehicles. The attraction of the whole operation is speed. This has led to the provision of unobstructed vehicle decks with a drive through capability. This configuration is extremely efficient for the purpose for which it was designed but it brought in its wake the problem of total lack of subdivision above the bulkhead deck.

This is in contradiction of Rule 24 of the 1984 PSC & S Regulations. Accordingly these Regulations require that the margin line of Ro-Ro passenger ferries must not become submerged at any time during flooding as well as at the final stage of flooding.

Ro-Ro passenger ferries are regarded essentially as passenger ships and are governed by the same Regulations for intact and damaged conditions. This approach is exemplified by a reply given by Mr. Taggart.

Q. Would it be right to say that the basic criteria of intact and damaged conditions have evolved from considerations of passenger ships generally?

A. That is correct. The only qualification is that the U.K. Regulations depart from the SOLAS Requirements in requiring that the bulkhead deck, the margin line, should not be immersed at any stage during intermediate and final stages of flooding.

It should be noted that currently this requirement for non-submersion of the margin line at any time during flooding is not universally accepted or applied. There is a real possibility that ships trading to the United Kingdom under foreign flag may not be capable of complying, in this respect, with the United Kingdom Regulations.

Mr. Taggart also gave evidence regarding the involvement of I.M.O. in Ro-Ro passenger ferry regulation.

This evidence was disturbing:–

"To the best of my knowledge I.M.O. has never undertaken work specifically directed towards passenger Ro-Ro ships as a type, in the various sub-committees concerned with passenger ship safety".

It is to the credit of the United Kingdom Administration that they have directed their attention towards Ro-Ro passenger ferries and have submitted papers to I.M.O. pressing for their regulation.

While it may have become conventional to regard Ro-Ro passenger ferries as passenger ships carrying cargo, it would be more logical to regard them as cargo ships carrying passengers. Their design is dominated by the freight vehicles and not by the passengers. In conventional passenger vessels Regulation 24 states:

> "All reasonable and practicable measures should be taken to limit
> where necessary the entry and spread of water above the bulkhead
> deck, such measures may include partial bulkheads or webs."

Because of the presence of these partial bulkheads or webs, the conventional passenger ship is permitted under the United Kingdom Regulations to submerge the margin line during intermediate stages of flooding provided the margin line is not submerged at the final stage. This is the sole distinction drawn between a conventional passenger ship and a Ro-Ro passenger ferry.

If substantial quantities of water reach the bulkhead deck, such a ferry may become totally unstable. The disaster to the *HERALD* was certainly unusual and it is to be hoped will never recur. Nevertheless, leaving the bow doors open is only one of several ways by which water in quantity may gain access to the bulkhead deck.

In the case of the ferry *WAHINE*, the ship grounded and heavily damaged the bottoms of several compartments below the vehicle deck. The ship eventually anchored in deeper water with the water line well above the vehicle deck but with the ship stable and the doors and scuppers holding well against the external water pressure. Water from the damaged compartments spread upwards through air pipes onto the vehicle deck and eventually free surface effects reduced the large positive metacentric height to the point where the ship became unstable and rolled over. This was an unusual type of accident, although repetition is not impossible.

The most likely cause for the entry of substantial quantities of water onto the vehicle deck must be side damage resulting from a collision, either with another vessel or with a fixed object such as a protruding jetty. Cross-channel ferries operate in a "high risk" environment, as, of necessity, many have to cross the main shipping lanes. In general they have a good record of collision-free voyages, but the risk of collision is always present and the consequences could be disastrous.

For the purposes of safety calculations the assumed extent of side damage which a ship can survive has been laid down for many years. The 1948 Convention postulated a length of 3.05 m + 0.03 L or 10.67 m whichever was less. The current requirement is 3.00 m + 0.03 L or 11 m or 10% of the length of the ship, whichever is the least. For the *HERALD* this rule would lead to assumed damage at the deepest subdivision draught of 6.90 m in length – a substantial figure. Transversely this damage must be taken as extending 20% of the breadth inboard from the ship's side at the deepest subdivision waterline and, from the 1960 Convention on, this damage must extend from the baseline upwards without limit. The worst case must be taken into account, perhaps that of a double bottom not being breached and thus providing buoyancy at a low level.

With a conventional Ro-Ro passenger ferry the transverse penetration of B/5 is of importance only below the bulkhead deck. Once the shell is penetrated above the bulkhead deck breaching is total.

As to the behaviour of the ship during flooding, there are a number of criteria which have to be met in the United Kingdom Regulations. The Department provided extensive evidence on this subject as well as a resume of the discussions and negotiations taking place in IMO in an attempt to secure uniformity of interpretation of certain parts of the 1974 amendments to the SOLAS Convention. This referred particularly to Regulation 8, which concerns a minimum acceptable standard of residual stability after damage. The damage stability criteria are currently considered under the two headings of 'Symmetrical' and 'Unsymmetrical'. In the 1965, 1980 and 1984 Regulations it is recognised that where a ship is fitted with decks, inner skins or longitudinal bulkheads of sufficient tightness to restrict the flow of water this should be taken into account.

For symmetrical flooding the 1960 Convention required a positive residual metacentric height of at least 50 mm in the final stage. This requirement remains current in the 1984 Regulations.

Angle of heel during symmetrical flooding is of considerable importance. In the 1952 Rules the requirements of the 1948 Convention were adopted and later embodied in the 1965 Rules. The margin line could be submerged but:

> if so "the construction of the ship shall be such as it will enable the Master to ensure:–
>
> (1) that the maximum angle of heel during any stage of such flooding will not be such as will endanger the safety of the ship; and
>
> (2) that the margin line will not be submerged in the final stage of flooding."

This then was the position following introduction of the 1965 Rules. In the 1980 PSC Regulations this was changed. Submersion of the margin line at intermediate stages of flooding was forbidden unless there was partial subdivision above the bulkhead deck which would limit heel to 20°. However for Ro-Ro ferries, i.e. where vehicles were to be carried on the bulkhead deck the margin line was not to be submerged at intermediate stages of flooding. This is the current Regulation. As regards the final stage of flooding the requirements have not changed since the 1948 Convention which simply states that the margin line must not be submerged in the final stage of flooding and that there must be a positive residual metacentric height of at least 50 mm.

For unsymmetrical flooding no consideration was given to submerging the margin line until the 1980 Regulations which introduced requirements paralleling those for symmetrical flooding and remain applicable.

As regards angle of heel with unsymmetrical flooding, the current requirement is that after the final stage and after equalisation the heel is not to exceed 7° and the margin line should not be submerged. This is the same as the 1965 Rules which, however, were more rigorous than the 1960 International Convention.

Residual stability with both symmetrical and unsymmetrical flooding is important. It is covered by the 1984 Regulations. A requirement was introduced in the 1980 Regulations that in all cases and at all stages there should be sufficient positive stability. In 1984 this was extended by requiring that the range of stability was to be to the satisfaction of the Department. This seems rather nebulous, but in practice the Department works to two standards:–

1. In the intermediate stages of flooding there must be a residual GZ of at least 0.03 m in association with a minimum range of 5°.

2. In the final stage of flooding the corresponding figures must be 0.05 m and 7°.

In the 1965 Rules the situation was much less specific – unsymmetrical flooding to be kept to a minimum – maximum heel before equalisation should not endanger the safety of the ship – equalisation to be completed in 15 minutes.

It will be seen that the current requirements applying to Ro-Ro passenger ferries fall into two categories. The first is for ships built under the 1965 Passenger Ship Rules which have, in particular, substantially lower standards of intermediate residual stability. The second category is for ships built under the 1980 or 1984 Regulations.

46. *Calculation of stability in the damaged condition*

The calculations that are required for sinkage, avoidance of margin line submersion and residual stability after damage are carried out by applying the statutory damage at various places along the length of the ship and then computing the sinkage, the stability, etc. at various stages of flooding.

If the ship is to meet one compartment standard then this damage is applied inside the length of each compartment. Clearly if the damage occurs on a bulkhead then two compartments will flood and this is not applicable to the one compartment ship calculation. It does, however, apply where a two compartment standard of subdivision is required. Similarly, of course, if a "three compartment" standard is required then three compartments must be assumed to be damaged. Clearly the likelihood of three compartment damage is much less then two or one compartment damage.

The calculations are carried out assuming permeabilities for the various damaged compartments. These are laid down in the PSC Rules. (Permeability is the percentage of the volume or waterplane of a space not occupied by its permanent contents.) The sinkage of the vessel is calculated together with any heel, either interim or final. The final metacentric height and the GZ values are also calculated. Currently these figures are derived for several intermediate stages of flooding and the values obtained compared with those required by the Regulations.

If a Ro-Ro passenger ferry does not submerge the margin line assuming any position of the damage and at any stage of the calculation and if the various requirements regarding residual stability and heel are met then the vessel is regarded as complying with the Regulations.

These calculations are necessary as a comparative measure — ship against ship — and as a means of implementing basic minimum standards. However, it is questionable whether they are a realistic absolute measure of the survivability of a Ro-Ro ferry in normal seagoing conditions. For a conventional passenger ship, the calculation is fairly realistic, because partial or total subdivision above the bulkhead deck undoubtedly will prevent water from spreading as it can in a vehicle ferry.

47. *I.M.C.O. Regulations 1974*

The I.M.C.O. Regulations on Subdivision and Stability of Passenger Ships 1974 were introduced as a full alternative to the deterministic Regulations of National Administrations. Owners and builders may opt for one or the other.

The I.M.C.O. Regulations comment upon aspects of this situation. In Part 1 — General Principles (page 41), the following statements are made:-

> "The 1960 Safety Convention Regulations therefore, in the main do not take into account evolution in ship design and advances in knowledge over about the past 50 years."

> "Ship design has changed considerably since then and with the passage of time the present method has become less meaningful as regards safety . . . ."

> "Improvements in machinery design have permitted higher power within less space. There has been a demand for more spacious passenger accommodations causing them to be located to a greater degree above the bulkhead deck. In consequence the safety standard applied to a ship whose primary function is the carriage of passengers has depreciated . . . ."

> "These and some other deficiencies of the Regulations in the 1960 Safety Convention lead to an incorrect estimate of the ship's safety . . . ."

On page 55 there is the following statement:-

> "Sub-Paragraph 5(c)(i) takes the place of Regulation 7(f) of Chapter II of the 1960 Safety Convention. Principally, it corrects the weakness

in that Regulation which permits acceptance of conditions wherein a damaged ship simultaneously might have only 2 inches (or 0.05 m) metacentric height and only 3 inches (or 0.076 m) freeboard, or other unrealistically low values despite the fact that chances of surviving such a condition, are as is shown in Fig. 2.6, non-existent."

These positive statements by I.M.O. cause the Court concern. In 1974 there was a further Convention but the basic position regarding positive residual GM and margin line freeboard was not changed. The 1965 Rules required a positive residual GM of at least 50 mm at the final stage of flooding. This was repeated in the 1980 and 1984 Regulations. The 1960 Convention, the 1965 rules, the 1974 Convention, the 1980 and 1984 Regulations all require the margin line not to be submerged (leaving a freeboard of 0.076 m).

Calculations made by the Department for the *HERALD* showed, that if damaged in some of the two compartment conditions in the Stability Book, with initial trim, the margin line would be on the waterline. It is more than likely that the same would apply for many other Ro-Ro passenger ferries.

That being so, the very conditions envisaged by I.M.O. on page 55 of their regulations can occur and are acceptable under the current PSC Regulations. Yet I.M.O. states "the chances of surviving such a condition are non-existent". **This conflict between I.M.O. and other Regulations should be investigated and clarified as a matter of urgency.**

48. *Survivability in a seaway*

Mr. Taggart gave evidence regarding the validity of these basic damage calculations in the context of an accident with a modest sea running. He was asked about this in the context of two compartment damage and 1½ m waves:-

A.   Again it is valid to the extent that it is setting an achievable standard in this respect. There are so many variables.

That answer is perfectly fair. There has to be an achievable standard and a means of comparative evaluation. However, Mr. Taggart went on to state:

> "My personal view is that the way forward is the provision of some other protection. Like you, I am concerned about the possibility of the scenario you envisage. I prefer to go forward looking at some form of protection on the vehicle deck taking the widest possible way to give maximum freedom to designers."

Q.   Would the liability of getting water onto the vehicle deck be reduced by having extra freeboard?

A.   Yes. Unless the freeboard is significant my preference is for some other arrangement which does not affect the cost of the ship and the commercial operation of the ship to the same extent and yet provides me with an even greater reserve.

All measures to improve survivability, whether internal or external, will affect the cost of the ship to some extent. **However the court does not accept that increasing the freeboard would necessarily affect the commercial operation of a Ro-Ro ferry significantly.**

Mr Rogan, a Naval Architect who is a consultant to the Sealink Organisation, gave evidence on the same point, namely the likelihood of water getting into the vehicle deck in large quantities in the event of damage as assumed and sinkage to the margin line in way of the damage.

Q.   Is it likely that a large quantity of water will go into that space, the vehicle deck, from the tops of the waves (and I am talking of a large quantity) through this 36ft long gash?

A.   It would seem probable.

Q. And if it does get in — and we are talking probably of the order of three figures of weight — is it going to affect the stability of the ship?

A. I would think yes.

Mr. Rogan referred to the I.M.O. Regulations on Subdivision and Stability of Passenger Ships. Section 4 of Part III gives a method of determining the probability that a damaged ship will not capsize and sink. A method is given in the Regulations for determining the critical significant wave height, at which the vessel would capsize, in terms of the effective freeboard after damage and the effective metacentric height flooded. This is embodied in graphs which show whether the ship would capsize with varying freeboards and significant wave heights.

Model tests were carried out on a Sealink short voyage vehicle ferry, 111 m in length. The freeboard of 0.076 m in the graphs corresponds to the distance from the margin line to the bulkhead deck. With this freeboard and an effective metacentric height of 1.5 m the critical significant wave height for this ship was 1 m. For an effective flooded metacentric height of 1 m the critical significant wave height was ½ m.

On the other hand for 1 m freeboard, for this ship, and 1.5 m effective flooded metacentric height there would be no possibility of the ship capsizing. Even at ½ m effective metacentric height the critical significant wave height would be 4 m.

Such waves do not represent unusual conditions. Standard wave frequency data for the Dover Straits covering 33 years show that in January, 75% of all waves exceeded ½ m and 55% exceeded 1 m. In March, the corresponding figures were 64% and 44%. In June, 49% and 30%. In September, 58% and 41%. Finally, in November, 81% of all waves exceeded ½ m and 65% of all waves exceeded 1 m.

As required by the Regulations the residual GM may be as low as 0.05 m. The residual GZ and range of stability are also very small. The amount of water on the vehicle deck that would destroy these small values is likely to be modest.

Furthermore, the effect of wind heel is not taken into account in the Regulations. With a high sided ferry with this level of residual stability even a moderate beam wind would tend to submerge both the margin line and the bulkhead deck edge.

The Court concludes that while the standard flooding calculation is necessary and valuable for comparative purposes, it must not be regarded as giving an absolute measure of the survivability of a damaged Ro-Ro passenger ferry in realistic seagoing conditions. **From this simple point of view alone, namely, water from waves getting onto the bulkhead deck in the event of a collision, the freeboard from the margin line to the vehicle deck should be increased for such ships to, perhaps, a minimum of 1 m.**

The Court also heard evidence from Mr Taggart as to calculations based on the simplified assumption that for the *HERALD* the vehicle decks should be considered without sheer but without increasing the height of the bow or the stern, or raising the margin line. This produced a distance from the existing margin line to bulkhead deck of 1.076 m which gave an improvement 4.5° in the angle to submerge the margin line amidships. The freeboard from the water line in the final stage of flooding was 1.15 m, the positive residual range of stability just under 11° and the maximum GZ in association with that range 0.094 m. Thus this change would give reasonable results in terms of both the range of damage stability and residual GZ but the most important effect would be upon the sheer survivability of the vessel in other than calm conditions. There would also be real benefit in the dynamic situation immediately following initial impact in a collision.

The Court recommends that detailed investigations and model tests should be carried out with a view to increasing the required distance from the margin line to the bulkhead deck in new design Ro-Ro passenger ferries to perhaps 1 m. The model tests should be ballasted to give the waterline at the margin over a range of 'damage' positions fore and aft and with the relevant openings in the superstructure representing statutory damage. Tests should be run in irregular sea conditions for significant wave heights. **The present definition of the margin line (76 mm below the bulkhead deck) derives from conventional passenger ships and has no inherent relevance to ships with no subdivision above the bulkhead deck. It should not apply to them.**

49. *Ships built under the 1960 Convention and the 1965 (PSC) Rules*

In terms of subdivision below the bulkhead deck these ships are deficient against the 1980 and 1984 Regulations for ferries. First, the requirement that the margin line must not be submerged at intermediate stages of flooding is not obligatory for ships built under the 1965 rules. It is permitted, provided that the construction ensures that the maximum angle of heel does not endanger the ship. Such submersion, even in ideal conditions, may lead to a greater likelihood of water entering the vehicle deck. Second, the requirement under the 1980 and 1984 Regulations that in all cases and at all stages sufficient positive residual stability must be provided and the range of stability to be to the satisfaction of the Administration does not apply. Many of these ships have a poor range of stability in the damaged condition while there is no requirement as to intermediate positive residual stability apart from the final stage GM requirement of 0.05 m minimum. Indeed ships built under the 1965 (PSC) Rules are likely to have negative residual stability at some intermediate stages of flooding, relying upon quick flooding to arrive at the stable final stage. Once a considerable quantity of water is present on its vehicle deck a 1965 Rules ferry is no more likely to capsize due to free surface than a 1984 Regulations ship. But the likelihood of the water getting there is greater, as is that of capsize due to lack of intermediate stage residual stability.

Immediate consideration should be given to phasing out vessels built under the 1965 rules unless they meet or can be modified to meet, at least, the 1980 standards in these respects, as they may be substantially less safe than modern ships. If they do not meet them and cannot be so modified, a finite and short term should be put on their lives.

50. *Future design considerations*

As described, an increase in the distance between the margin line and the bulkhead deck will decrease the possibility of substantial quantities of water gaining access to the vehicle deck in transient collision conditions and in a seaway. Alternatively there are lines of investigation that should be pursued urgently with the object of finding methods of improving the survivability of Ro-Ro passenger ferries.

50.1 The vehicle deck may be subdivided transversely by permanent bulkheads with doors. This method would bring a Ro-Ro ferry into conformity with Rule 24 of the 1984 Regulations. The ship would then parallel normal passenger ship construction.

However, such transverse bulkheads, if permanent, even with doors, could constitute a grave penalty against the commercial operation of a ferry for its primary purpose. It is concluded that a feasibility exercise should be carried out to investigate the practical details of such divisions and their effect upon commercial operations. In the case of train ferries this method would be prohibitive. Trains are loaded in rakes and then compressed against buffers. No transverse division whether permanent with doors or portable could be accepted.

The Court heard evidence from Mr. Taggart illustrating the potential effect of **transverse bulkheads** on the *HERALD*. Three bulkheads above the bulkhead deck were envisaged. Damage was assumed alternatively in way of two of these bulkheads. Considerable improvements resulted. Undoubtedly transverse bulkheads in the vehicle deck would effect a considerable improvement in the safety of these vessels, but the thrust of any investigation must be directed towards operational practicability.

50.2 An alternative possibility for subdividing the vehicle deck would be to fit **portable transverse bulkheads.** In one form these could be top or side hinged doors. Such bulkheads are fitted to deep sea Ro-Ro freight vessels. However with deep sea vessels the need for a minimal turnround time is not as pressing as with short sea ferries, especially on routes such as Dover/Calais. Loading has to proceed sequentially from the far end of the ship towards the ramp and this may introduce trim problems. Portable transverse bulkheads would increase the turn-round time and result in a small loss of stowage space.

Alternative types of portable bulkheads could be envisaged, perhaps vertically sliding, housing below the bulkhead deck; but these would only be possible in the event that the bulkhead deck was not a strength deck. Other possibilities, such as vertical roller shutter bulkheads or alternatively sideways rolling shutter bulkheads should be investigated.

A detailed study should be made of all possible types of portable bulkheads, both structurally and in terms of their practical effects including concomitant vehicle stowing disadvantages as mentioned above. If fitted, either these or transverse bulkheads with doors could afford a major increase in the survivability of Ro-Ro passenger ferries. It is conceivable that arrangements could be developed to keep loss of space and vehicle handling time within acceptable limits.

50.3   Another possibility is to divide the vehicle deck with side longitudinal bulkheads, the space outboard of these being themselves subdivided transversely. The Court heard evidence on this proposal. This was in the context of the *HERALD* herself. The inboard side of the line of casings was on the B/5 line in the midships area. Bulkheads were envisaged extending fore and aft until reaching the forward and aft compartments, with three transverse bulkheads in the main length of each outboard space. Suitable access doors were postulated.

On the assumption that two compartment damage did not penetrate the B/5 bulkhead, the result was a range of stability and GZ giving full compliance with all the required damage criteria. This proposal is practicable and satisfactory in the context of a vessel with twin casings. It would not be applicable to vessels with centreline casings. The arrangement would be likely to be dangerous should damage penetrate beyond the B/5 line. Mr. Rogan introduced evidence from 1974 I.M.O. Regulations on subdivision and stability concerning the statistics of damage penetration from 296 penetrations. This indicated that approximately 45% of penetrations exceeded the B/5 line. Mr. Rogan gave his opinion that this could produce a more dangerous situation than would have existed without the longitudinal bulkheads. The Court agrees with this view.

However the proposal has some attractions and there is an urgent need for investigations into the effect of longitudinal bulkheads on a range of vessels. These investigations should include depth of penetration probability statistics and a definition of the risks involved with different configurations and penetrations.

50.4   A further concept is to supply either permanent or portable buoyancy external to the hull proper. Permanent external buoyancy could be in the form of sponsons of suitable shape, extending from below the lightest waterline to a level well above the bulkhead deck. In the event of collision, a sponson would be penetrated in way of the collision point but the bulk of sponson volume would remain intact, supplying both buoyancy and effective intact waterplane. There should therefore be a high degree of internal transverse subdivision limiting the loss of buoyancy to a small fore and aft extent around the damage.

The effect of such sponsons on survivability could be very beneficial, but they would produce some difficulties. The breadth of the vessel could be increased and with it the metacentric height, while the deployment of lifeboats would be seriously affected. A real advantage of such a system is that it could be applicable to existing vessels, and of particular advantage to those built under the 1965 (rules).

50.5   Inflatable flotation collars stowed inside the line of the shell can be envisaged, giving somewhat the same effect as sponsons. As with sponsons the range of stability and survivability after damage could be increased considerably by such arrangement.

51. *Downflooding*

In conjunction with all such arrangements, detailed consideration should be given to access openings from the vehicle deck. Casings and trunks usually contain staircases leading down to spaces below the bulkhead deck and up either to another vehicle deck or to accommodation. In the *HERALD* casualty the first indication of trouble was water coming down the stairs into the forward drivers' accommodation. There was little to stop water going into the lower levels of accommodation.

This point was underlined by Mr. Taggart in his evidence about attempts to obtain agreement on Regulation 8 of the 1974 Amendments to *SOLAS* Convention. Questioned regarding the residual range of stability and the contrast between the maximum heel figure of 7° proposed by the United Kingdom and others as against the 20° proposed by the U.S.A. and the U.S.S.R., Mr. Taggart said that to achieve the latter angle would be extremely difficult.

> "I would think to achieve 20° in most vessels there are so many problems in passenger vessels with accesses within the ship to below decks that effectively your curve is terminated because of progressive flooding problems well before 20° of heel. That is not 20° angle of heel from upright; that is 20° from the equilibrium position . . . So that you are talking about possibly 27° or more. You would require to keep all your openings safe so that no progressive flooding could occur within say 27°. It would be a major problem . . . It is most important in these things not to impose criteria which are impossible to achieve."

It should not be very difficult in Ro-Ro passenger ferries to ensure major improvements in these respects. Sill heights should be increased appreciably. **Wherever possible access to spaces such as the engine room and below bulkhead deck passenger accommodation should be without intermediate access to the bulkhead deck.** Exits in the casings from this vehicle deck should lead only upwards. Access to below bulkhead deck spaces, except where through watertight doors kept shut at sea, should be from the deck above the bulkhead deck.

The Court does not agree that it would be a major problem to achieve substantially higher downflooding angles. It would seem to be relatively easy and achievable even on many existing vessels. Immediate attention should be given to this point.

52. *Air pipes and vehicle deck drainage.*

At least two ferry disasters have been connected with flooding through air pipes. In the *PRINCESS VICTORIA* there was flooding down air pipes to compartments below the vehicle deck. In the case of *WAHINE* there was flow upwards from flooded spaces below the bulkhead deck and onto it via air pipe grilles which could not be closed.

Following the *PRINCESS VICTORIA* casualty a number of new ships were fitted with air pipes which did not vent directly at near bulkhead deck level but instead went either to the deck above or near to the underside of the deck above and back down towards the level of the vehicle bulkhead deck. If such measures had been adopted in the *WAHINE* the ship might well have survived, bad though the damage was. It is highly desirable that there should be general requirement of this nature. Similar attention should be paid to sounding pipes.

Similarly, if the overboard scuppers from the bulkhead deck are required to be remotely controlled they should be operable from the bridge. Ferries may capsize very rapidly and it is possible that there will not be time for a manual opening of these valves.

Inboard drains to centreline dump tanks are a requirement for Ro-Ro cargo ferries following the *HERO* disaster. This first appeared in the British Cargo Ship Construction and Survey Rules, 1980 and was recommended by I.M.O. under Resolution A515(13) of November 1983, but not as a requirement.

For Ro-Ro passenger ferries the Department introduced in 1984 a regulation requiring inboard drainage to dump tanks where the bulkhead deck is submerged at a heel of 5° or less. Further, the Department is in favour of pumped drainage from the vehicle deck at rates of 600–700 tonnes per hour.

Mr. Rogan gave evidence that to fit such dump tanks with large stripping pumps would amount to an exercise in 'pumping the ocean dry'. While the limitations of this proposal can be seen in an extreme case, such as the *HERALD* accident, nevertheless such systems are highly desirable in order to cope with water entering the vehicle deck, perhaps from waves lapping over side damage with small residual freeboard. The quantities involved in such circumstances could be of the order of several hundred tons per hour and, if so, the deck could be kept drained by dump tanks with suitable overboard stripping pumps. There are such installations at present in service.

There should be a requirement for such a system for Ro-Ro passenger ferries with dedicated pumps capable of stripping at a rate of at least 600 tons per hour. Desirably such pumps should be of the same order of capacity as heeling tank pumps with a capacity of perhaps 1200–1500 tons per hour. The drain valves should be remotely controlled from the bridge.

Miscellaneous

53. *Uniformity of interpretation of Regulation 8 1974 Amendments to SOLAS Convention*

The Court heard evidence about discussions in progress at I.M.O. regarding a minimum acceptable standard of residual stability after damage in terms or Regulation 8. Under Regulation 8.2.3 – Range of Stability in the Final Stage – the United Kingdom, the Netherlands and the Federal Republic of Germany have proposed a maximum GZ of at least 0.05 m and a residual range of stability not less than 7°. However, the U.S.A., the U.S.S.R., Poland and Norway all favour a maximum GZ of at least 0.10 m and a residual range of not less than 20°, although the U.S.A. later retracted to 14°. It is the opinion of the Department that the U.S.A./U.S.S.R., proposals are impracticable and would gravely impair commercial viability of the ferries.

The Working Group is considering two alternatives. Alternative 1, a maximum of at least 0.10 m and a residual range not less than 15° with an area under the curve of not less than 0.020 m radians. (This is provided that the ship has sufficient residual stability to withstand passenger movement and LSA deployment). Alternative 2, a maximum GZ of at least 0.05 m with a residual range not less than 7° and an area under the curve of not less than 0.003 m/radians. (This is provided that LSA deployment and wind heel moment are to be considered).

There are considerable differences between Alternatives 1 and 2, the latter being the UK/NL/FRG proposal. The effect of Alternative 1 upon the design viability of Ro-Ro passenger ferries should be examined quantitatively in detail to see whether the Department is correct as to the possible effects. The effect of wind heel moments should be taken into account.

Regulation 8.5 – Maximum Heel Before Equalisation – leads to no disagreement. Both Alternatives envisage 15° of heel. The UK/NL/FRG proposed that the margin line on ferries should not be submerged. The U.S.A. agrees. The two Alternatives, in addition to 15° maximum heel, require non-submergence of the margin line in Ro-Ro type vessels.

Regulation 8.6.2 – Heel in the Final Condition – does not appear to offer any particular problems. However Regulation 8.6.3 does. This covers stability in intermediate stages of flooding. The Working Group is considering two alternatives:–

Alternative 1

Maximum GZ of at least 0.05 m in association with a residual range of 7°

Alternative 2

Maximum GZ of at least 0.03 m and a residual range of at least 5°.

The main difference between Alternatives 1 and 2 is in the residual stability in intermediate stages as well as in the final stage of flooding.

The present situation cannot be regarded as satisfactory. **Clearly it is of the utmost importance that new unified minimum standards be adopted as soon as possible.** Unilateral action by the United Kingdom would be unwise in view of the possibility that eventually I.M.O. might adopt Alternative 1 rather than the U.K. sponsored Alternative 2.

Evidence presented at this Investigation indicated that well in excess of 20,000,000 passengers use ferry services to and from the United Kingdom in a year. It is thus of over-riding importance to the U.K. Government and to the travelling public that the international regulatory position be rationalised and a uniform standard agreed. A considerable number of the ferries operating around the United Kingdom do not come under the jurisdiction of the Department.

After resolution of the choice between Alternatives 1 and 2 upon ferry design and viability, the United Kingdom should press I.M.O. for:–

> (a) **Increased distance from margin line to bulkhead deck for Ro-Ro passenger ferries, or**
>
> (b) **The provision of some degree of subdivision of the vehicle deck, or alternatively the provision of non-destructible external waterplane area and buoyancy.**

54. *Research*

The Court was presented with details of a proposed research programme agreed between the General Council of British Shipping and the Department aimed at improvement of Ro-Ro safety and, in particular, of subdivision and stability. The programme will be funded by the Industry and will be controlled by a Steering Committee consisting of the Surveyor General of the Department, the Deputy Surveyor General, Chief Ship Surveyor of Lloyd's Register and the Director (Marine Services) of GCBS. The Committee will have additionally not more than two co-opted members.

The work will be carried out by a team drawn from:–

> Three Quays Marine Services Limited
> Hart Fenton & Company Limited
> Lloyd's Register of Safety and Technology Department.

The work programme covers three principal areas where urgent research is required:–

1. Improvement in survival capability if water reaches a vehicle deck.

2. Further determination of required level of stability for vessel survival in the event of damage.

3. Changes likely to be necessary to Ro-Ro vessel design in the light of proposed legislative changes.

There is a fourth area which is apparently missing namely:–

> Improvement in the prevention of water reaching the vehicle deck in the event of damage occurring in realistic seagoing conditions.

The latter area is as important as the other three and logically should precede them.

This point carries over to Task 4, namely survival capability. The tank test programme should cover a wide spectrum of possibilities such as the systematic testing of survivability in waves, with varying distances from the margin line to the bulkhead deck and the provision of external add-on buoyancy. In particular the validity of the present survival criteria should be checked experimentally, in a range of irregular significant sea heights with the enclosed superstructure opened by side damage.

It should be emphasised that this Formal Investigation is into the disaster to the *HERALD* and into possible means of improving the safety and survivability of Ro-Ro passenger ferries. In this context Task 1 should concentrate on Ro-Ro passenger ferries. It is essential that all calculations, including those for residual stability and freeboard, should be in the context of a range of initial trims.

The casualty analysis and relative safety proposals appear to have been covered largely by the Norwegian submission to I.M.O. submitted in evidence during the *HERALD* Investigation (November 1983 Paper SLF/20). Between the evidence based upon Lloyd's Register's work and the Norwegian paper, this section would appear to be largely unnecessary. It is difficult to see how the relative safety of new Ro-Ro ships can be compared statistically with existing ships. Risk assessment is also likely to be upon an inadequate statistical basis.

This study does not appear to cover actual tank testing but finishes by preparing specifications for a programme of tests. Thus it seems unlikely that there will be any tank test information available for the September 1987 meeting of the SLF Sub-Committee of I.M.O. It is considered that the tests should impose statutory damage through portable side plates in the superstructure located at, say, midships and near the quarter points. The model should then be ballasted so that

> (a) the waterline is at the margin in way of the 'damage' location for any given distance between margin line and bulkhead deck.

(b)   that the metacentric height is adjusted to be alternatively 0.05 m or 0.10 m; and

(c)   finally, that the vessel be tested statically on a number of headings in irregular sea conditions using a suitable spectrum with a range of significant waveheights.

Finally, no target date for the completion of a model test programme is given. It is of considerable importance that this be as soon as physically possible in view of the need to consider the effects of the results upon ferry design.

It is essential that the research programme convince Government and the Public that its conclusions are objective and at arm's length from purely commercial considerations.

In particular, the merit rating mentioned in 2.4.4. and 2.5.3 of the programme, requires clarification as to its nature. Is it, for example, to be an operator's assessment of least possible inconvenience or is it to apply strictly to the safety of the vessel or will it be based upon an objective combination of these and other aspects?

55. *Management changes since the disaster*

In 1985 Mr. Barrett became the General Manager of P. & O. European Transport Services Fleet Management Limited and was appointed a director of that company in 1986. He is well qualified nautically and, as such, is responsible for navigational and safety matters. He is also a member of the British Delegation to the I.M.O. Committees concerned with Roll on/Roll off shipping matters.

On Tuesday, 12th May 1987, Mr. Barrett was appointed a director of Townsend Thoresen Limited and given responsibility to continue the review of safety and nautical procedures. It was discovered that some vessels could close their bow and stern doors while on the berth and others could not. Instructions were given to the Master of those vessels which could close their doors while on the berth to do so in future. The Masters of those vessels which could not close their doors at the berth were instructed to do so as soon as the appropriate modifications to the ships or to their berths had been carried out. By the middle of May Mr. Barrett had made certain changes to the Company's Standing Orders. In particular he had deleted what has been called the "negative reporting" element. Masters were left in no doubt that their ships should not leave their berths until the Master had received a positive report from an officer that the bow doors or stern doors, as the case may be, were closed. Instructions have been given to all ships to this effect.

Mr. Barrett told the Court that in the near future he intends to carry out a number of further steps including the issue to all ships of the fleet of one set of Regulations. These will make for uniformity of practice throughout the ships of the fleet. Such orders would not inhibit Masters from issuing orders which they regard as urgently required for the running of their own ships.

Mr. Barrett is also seeking the design of log books with a format which can be common to all ships. Further consideration is to be given as to whether there is a need for three deck officers in addition to the Master on Spirit class vessels on the Zeebrugge run. Mr. Barrett is looking into the question as to how Company orders and other important information and advice can be disseminated effectively throughout the fleet. He is reviewing the structure of management and making recommendations to the Chairman. In particular he is considering the desirability of allocating specifically to one man all questions relating to matters of safety. He also has in mind the important question: to whom and by what manner should Masters communicate with shore management? He is in favour of having a man with nautical qualifications in the shore organisation. The evidence given during this formal investigation strongly supports that view. Matters such as draught readings, determination and control of dead weight and stability, all of which as Mr. Barrett noted, gave rise to discussions during the course of this investigation are areas of concern to him.

Reference is made to this evidence in the hope that Mr. Barrett's conclusions will bear fruit, and so that readers of this Report will be able to distinguish between the errors of the past and the hopes for the future.

It is apparent that the new top management has taken to heart the gravity of this catastrophe and the Company has shown a determination to put its house in order. This Court need **say no more than stress the need for:**

    (a) **Clear and concise orders.**

    (b) **Strict discipline.**

    (c) **Attention at all times to all matters affecting the safety of the ship and those on board. There must be no "cutting of corners".**

    (d) **The maintenance of proper channels of communication between ship and shore for the receipt and dissemination of information.**

    (e) **A clear and firm management and command structure.**

56. *Lifeboats*

The *HERALD* was classified as a passenger ship engaged on short international voyages with either a "one compartment" or "two compartment" standard of watertight subdivision. As a one compartment ship the number of crew and passengers carried was limited to the capacity of her lifeboats, that is to say 630. As a two compartment ship the total number carried could be increased to 1,400 of whom 770 were notionally allocated to liferafts. But the emergency procedures for dealing with the abandonment of a Class II passenger ship are based on three fundamental assumptions. they are:

    1.   That if the hull is breached, the ship will remain afloat in a nearly upright condition for at least 30 minutes and that the life-saving equipment located in both sides of the ship could be deployed. It is assumed, therefore, that it will be possible to use all, or nearly all, of the lifeboats and liferafts.

    2.   That all the lifeboats and liferafts could be launched within a period of 30 minutes and that there will be sufficient time to effect the abandonment.

    3.   That there will be a sufficient number of trained persons on board for mustering and assisting the passengers and that there will be a sufficient number of crew for launching and thereafter operating all the life-saving craft. This makes the assumption that there will be an orderly abandonment involving first the assembly of the passengers at the muster stations where the lifejackets will be issued and secondly that the public rooms will provide protection from the elements to the passengers while they are waiting to abandon ship.

It seems to the Court that these assumptions are not valid for Ro-Ro ferries.

Two recent casualties involving Ro-Ro ferries have shown that when the water-tight integrity of such ships has been lost there is a strong possibility that the ship will not remain upright for 30 minutes. It is the view of this Court that the time has now come when the whole philosophy of carrying lifeboats on ships which are never far from land should be reviewed by the International Maritime Organisation. This is a topic which requires much careful consideration before any International agreement is likely to be reached. The Court would, however, draw attention to three particular aspects of this question, two of which relate specifically to Ro-Ro ferries.

(1) All ferries have heavily constructed belting which protrudes from the ship's side. Although they have farings in way of the boat lowering positions the guard rails can catch the gunwales of a lifeboat, particularly if there is any sea running, and cause it to roll violently.

(2) The means of release gives rise to difficulty and sometimes to moments of danger, as for example if both ends are not released simultaneously, with the result that the boat is "hung up" at one end or the other. The heavy blocks are a danger to occupants of a boat as they swing to and fro on the ends of their falls.

(3) There was some evidence that the height of the embarkation deck should be as low as possible. There are practical reasons for this, but in an emergency it seems to be against human instincts to go to a lower deck than the one a person is on. Passengers are more likely to want to move to a higher deck. There are obvious advantages in drastically reducing the number of lifeboats carried and thereby saving space and reducing weight. In their place a large number of liferafts could be carried with advantage. The Court recommends that the Department should give a lead in initiating discussions.

57. *Official log books*

One matter which came to light during the Investigation was that false entries are made in official log books without detection. The draught of the *HERALD* was not read before sailing. Fictitious entries were made in her official log book. Those entries seen by the Court showed that the *HERALD* sailed from Zeebrugge on an even keel on every occasion. In truth the *HERALD* frequently sailed from Zeebrugge trimmed by the head. There was evidence from the Department that it has not been regarded as the best use of resources for a surveyor to read the official log-books which are sent ashore. The Court agrees that there would be a waste of skilled manpower involved in reading all official log books with an educated eye. This must be so. There is no obvious advantage in discovering errors long after the event. Furthermore there would be a strong temptation to make a false entry in the official log-book if the draught of a ship had been taken before sailing and if it revealed that the ship was marginally overloaded. It is most unlikely that such a false entry could be detected.

There should be a requirement that the departure draughts must be entered in the deck log book as well as the Official Log book. The only practical way of enforcing such a rule would be for the Department to initiate random spot checks and for there to be heavy penalties for an infringement of the Regulations. **The Court recommends that further consideration be given to this topic.**

58. *Reporting of accidents*

Captain J.J. de Coverly, who is a Principal Nautical Surveyor of the Department, drew to the attention of the Court the provisions of the Merchant Shipping (Safety Officials and Reporting of Accidents and Dangerous Occurrences) Regulations 1982 which imposes a duty on the Master of a ship to notify the Department of every dangerous occurrence on board. He expressed his view that the regulation as to what must be reported is too narrowly drawn. **Consideration should be given to enlarging that regulation to include every occurrence which is potentially hazardous to the ship or to any person on board.**

59. *Licensing of ferry operators*

Mr. Robert Owen, on behalf of the National Union of Seamen, raised the question whether there should be a system for licensing operators of passenger ferries. The purpose of introducing such a system could only be that it would enable the Department of Transport (1) to set standards for the safe operation of ferries, and (2) to monitor their management and operation. It was suggested that licences would be issued for a specific period of time and renewed only when Inspectors were satisfied that proper standards were being maintained. Such a system of licensing operators would have wide ramifications. The Court has not heard sufficient evidence to express any firm view upon it, but is conscious that the standards in many other industries have been improved by licensing. The court draws attention to this suggestion and expresses the hope that serious consideration will be given to it.

60. *Counsel to the Tribunal*

On the 3rd August 1984 there was published the Report of the Court which held a Formal Investigation into the circumstances attending the collision between the motor vessel *EUROPEAN GATEWAY* and the motor vessel *SPEEDLINK VANGUARD*. In the course of that Report the Court said:

> "This is not the first Wreck Inquiry at which an attack has been made upon the Department of Transport or its predecessor. We doubt if it will be the last. The wide responsibilities of the Department in the field of merchant shipping will often make it a natural target when a casualty occurs. When a party makes charges against the Department, counsel who has the conduct of the Inquiry is placed in a position of difficulty and embarrassment. The expedient adopted in the present case of instructing separate counsel to defend the position of the Department is not really satisfactory. Consideration should be given to this problem and, in particular, to the question of whether it would be preferable for a wreck inquiry to be conducted by counsel to the tribunal who is independent of the Department of Transport."

Quite recently the Secretary of State was asked what action had been taken in respect of the 15 recommendations made in the Report on the loss of the *EUROPEAN GATEWAY*. In answer to the recommendation quoted above he said:

> "When there appears to be a conflict of interest it is the Department's view that this can be met by appointing separate representation for the Department's Marine Directorate."

The Merchant Shipping (Formal Investigations) Rules 1985, under which a Formal Investigation is now conducted, make provision in Rule 5(1) which was intended to meet this point. Mr. David Steel Q.C. was instructed by the Treasury Solicitor to represent the Secretary of State. On his advice notice was served upon the Department, on whose behalf the Treasury Solicitor instructed Mr. Richard Stone Q.C. But that is not a satisfactory answer to the problem. Mr. Steel told the Court of his sense of unease because he received instructions from the Casualty Investigation Branch of the Department. He said "I have personally found it difficult to be satisified that I am, **and also appear to be,** acting in a sense in the public interest, quite distinct from any interest of the Department." After a reference by the Court to the anomaly that the Minister and his Department have been separately represented, Mr. Steel said "It is difficult for me to conceive and understand it, I should think it is even more difficult for the ordinary member of the public". The responsibilities of the Department for matters of safety of life at sea are very wide. After a casualty has occurred there is a natural instinct on the part of ship-owners to adopt the attitude that they had not taken certain precautions because the Department had not made Rules which required those precautions. From that defensive position there can easily develop what appears to the public, probably erroneously, to be a cover-up. The interest which the public has taken in this Investigation has become apparent from the very large number of letters which have been written to the Court. **In every Formal Investigation it is of great importance that members of the public should feel confident that a searching investigation has been held, that nothing has been swept under the carpet and that no punches have been pulled. Many problems relating to the investigation of shipping casualties are under active consideration. In the course of considering all the related problems, further consideration should be given to the question of appointing counsel to the tribunal, and *not* on behalf of the Secretary of State, so that he can be seen to be wholly independent of the Department.**

APPENDIX 1

List of Witnesses who gave oral evidence

1. Michael Charles Tracey, Carpenter

2. Leigh Cornelius, Able Seaman

3. Terence David Ayling, Boatswain

4. Stephen Robert Homewood, Assistant Purser

5. John Edward Butler, Steward in Drivers' accommodation

6. Philip Richard Naisbitt, Acting Quartermaster

7. Michael Ronald Mordue, 3rd Engineer

8. Nicholas Frank Ray, 2nd Engineer

9. Daniel Morgan-John, Able Seaman

10. Anthony George Down, Able Seaman

11. Edward Max Potterton, Seaman and Deck Storekeeper

12. Paul Cormack, Assistant Steward

13. Mark Anthony Squire, Able Seaman

14. Paul Ronald Morter, 2nd Officer

15. Mark Victor Stanley, Assistant Boatswain

16. Thomas Hume Wilson, A Quartermaster

17. Leslie Sabel, Chief Officer

18. Captain David Lewry, Master

19. Jeffrey Kenneth Develin, Director, Townsend Car Ferries

20. Captain Anthony de Ste Croix, Master, *PRIDE OF FREE ENTERPRISE*

21. Anthony Peter Young, Director, Townsend Car Ferries

22. Captain Robert-Paxton Blowers, *PRIDE OF CALAIS* (Previously Master *PRIDE OF FREE ENTERPRISE*

23. John Francis Alcindor, Deputy Chief Superintendent

24. Captain John Michael Kirby, Townsend Car Ferries Senior Master

25. Wallace James Ayers, Director, Townsend Car Ferries

26. Andrew Clifford Parker, Passenger

27. Vincent Derek Young Cochran, Chief Surveyor, London District

28. Roger Macdonald Taggart, Principal Ship Surveyor

29. John Calderwood, Passenger

30. Anthony Dennis Barrett, Director, P & O European Transport Services Fleet Management Ltd.

31. Peter John Ford, Chairman, North Sea Ferries Limited.

32. Dr. Ian Dand, Naval Architect

33. Kenneth Douglas Alexander Shearer, Principal Ship Surveyor

34.   Marshall Meek, Chief Naval Architect

35.   Professor Erik Skeneroth, Technical Director

36.   Captain Archibald Munro, Principal Nautical Surveyor

37.   Christopher William Fyans, Consultant Marine Surveyor

38.   William Alan Graham, Principal Engineering Surveyor

39.   Anthony James Rogan, Consultant Naval Architect

Depositions of the following witnesses were read

1.   Martin James Barnes, Steward

2.   Clive Arthur Bush, Assistant Steward

3.   Keith Richard Brown, 3rd Engineer

4.   Tony Roy Bushby, Assistant Steward

5.   Richard Martin Curner, Assistant Cook

6.   Nicholas William Delo, Crew Messman

7.   Henry Graham, Kiosk Steward

8.   Stephen John Greenaway, A.B.

9.   David Arthur Stoneham Hawken, Senior Steward

10.   Kenneth Hollingsbee, Assistant Steward

11.   John Leonard Hudson, Senior Barman

12.   John Kenneth Jackson, Assistant Steward

13.   Brian James Kendall, A.B.

14.   David George Matthews, Cashier

15.   Graham Merricks, Steward

16.   Charles Arthur Smith, Assistant Purser

17.   Michael Gordon Stickler, Assistant Steward

18.   Moyna Patricia Ellen Thompson, Senior Shop Stewardess

19.   David Tracey, Assistant Steward

20.   William Sean Walker, A.B.

21.   Paul Malcolm White, Chief Cook

22.   Daniel Wyman, Junior Catering Rating

23.   Elias Vanmore, Chief Mate of SANDERUS

24.   Dirk Wijdoodt, 2nd Mate of SANDERUS

25.   Patrick Struyf, Pipeman on SANDERUS

26.   Bernard G.M. Vandzandweghe, Loading Master

27.   Pierre Vuylsteke, Assistant Port Manager

28.   Captain John William Martin, Senior Master of *HERALD* 1980–1985

29.   John Richard Parsons, Accountant

30.   Anthony Colin Reynolds, Assistant Marine Superintendent

31.   John Edward Stevenson, Marine Administrator

32.   Ronald Ellison, Marine Superintendent

33.   Captain Edward Frank Ward

Statements of the following witnesses were read:

1,   Peter Ian Williamson, Passenger

2.   Terence David Smith, Passenger

3.   Stanley Mason, Passenger

4.   Andrew David Teare, Passenger

5.   Petar Zutic, Passenger

6.   Captain G.W. Budd, RIVER TAMAR

7.   Captain J.A.D. Scott, DUKE OF ANGLIA

8.   Richard Leslie Martin, General Manager, Zeebrugge

Letters from the following ten passengers were read:

1.   J.F. Newman

2.   J.S. Underhill

3.   G. Lamy

4.   A.K. Rogers

5.   D. Woodhouse

6.   J.P. Kay – Haulage

7.   M.A. Bennett

8.   D. Gudgeon

9.   S.C. Burbridge

10.   R. Summerfield

        and from the Assistant Chief Constable (Operations), Kent County Constabulary.

        There was also put in evidence a written Report from:

        Lloyd's Register Safety Technology Department.

APPENDIX II

Search and Rescue

When the *HERALD* capsized the tide was ebbing. The current in the channel outside the Mole was setting ENE about 1½ knots. The dredger *SANDERUS* was dredging inwards between the New and Old Mole on the Western side of the channel. She observed the ferry pass her at about 8 knots. Several of the *SANDERUS* crew confirm that the bow doors were open. At about 1828 the *SANDERUS* observed the *HERALD* sheering to starboard and heeling to port. Within 30 seconds the ferry's lights went out; she had capsized.

The *SANDERUS* informed Port Control Zeebrugge on VHF and immediately set out towards the scene of the accident. The *SANDERUS* must have been the first to arrive. She commenced searching for survivors. The Chief Mate mentions going alongside the casualty but there is no further account of her movements or activity.

The British coaster *RIVER TAMAR* was preparing to leave Zeebrugge at 1830 when Port Control informed her of the accident. The *RIVER TAMAR* proceeded at once to the wreck and after searching down tide for 15 minutes she went alongside. At about 1845 GMT two tugs from Zeebrugge *BURGERMEESTER VAN DAMME* and *SEA HORSE* also came alongside just aft of the funnels of the *HERALD*. By this time No. 1 LIFEBOAT from Zeebrugge had been launched and a control centre set up in the Pilot Station. Numerous small boats and fishing vessels were also searching the area for survivors. The Ro/Ro vessel *GABRIELLE WEHR* and the Townsend ferry *EUROPEAN TRADER* were despatched from Zeebrugge. The *GABRIELLE WEHR* anchored 3 cables West of the wreck, prepared a helipad on the upper deck, opened the stern ramp and prepared to receive casualties with the approval of the Rescue Centre. The *EUROPEAN TRADER* lowered a boat and searched the area to no avail, thereafter she anchored and later sent the Second Officer aboard the *HERALD* with the bosun, both of whom had knowledge of her layout, to assist in locating survivors.

The crane barge *ZEEBRUGGE I* was on scene at 1900 and subsequently was able to supply two divers, boats and gear. The tug *SEA LION* ferried survivors. The first Mayday Relay was transmitted by Ostende Radio at 1855 and this alerted Dover MRCC. At 1856 the *NORDIC FERRY* (Townsend) sailed from Zeebrugge to assist in the rescue. She supplied harnesses, an Aldis lamp and gear.

At 1910 the first Belgian Sea King was over the wreck and at 1925 the first Belgian diving team was aboard. The Ro/Ro ferry *DUKE OF ANGLIA* was approaching the Scheur Zand buoy on passage from Chatham to Zeebrugge when she picked up the Mayday Relay requesting all vessels' assistance. At 1955 she launched a lifeboat under the command of the Chief Officer with the Second Engineer, 3 A.B.s and the Cook. After searching round the wreck the Chief Officer observed lights on the upper car deck of the *HERALD*. The boat was manoeuvred into the stern area of the ship only to find that the lights were those of a lorry which had overturned. The boat was unable to proceed further due to cars blocking the entrance.

About 2000 *H.M.S. HURWORTH* in Ostende sent her divers by road to Zeebrugge and at 2020 *B.N.S. EKSTER* sailed from Zeebrugge with more divers. The R.N. Clearance Diving Centre at Portsmouth were alerted at this time.

At 2050 the *DUKE OF ANGLIA'S* Chief Officer made the decision to board the wreck, leaving the Second Engineer in charge of the boat secured to the tug *FIGHTER* which was alongside having arrived from Flushing.

Around 2100 most of the windows on the starboard side of the wreck which gave access to the passenger lounges had been broken and survivors were still being pulled out. Two British divers from *H.M.S. HURWORTH* arrived on the *HERALD* by helicopter. Twenty minutes later *H.NL.M.S. MIDDLEBURG* was in the vicinity.

At 2140 *BURGERMEESTER VAN DAMME* who had ferried survivors ashore was back alongside the *RIVER TAMAR* departed to Zeebrugge with many more on board. At 2153 a U.K. helicopter with 20 divers arrived at Zeebrugge.

At 2157 *B.N.S. KREKEL* sailed from Zeebrugge with divers. *B.N.S. CROCUS, VALCKE, ZEEMEEUW, BIJ* and *SPA* also supplied divers and personnel. At this time *FGS GOETTINGEN* and *H.M.S. HURWORTH* sailed from Ostende.

The situation at this time was very confused due to lack of lighting, the numbers of rescuers and helicopter noise which made voice communication aboard the wreck almost impossible.

During the next 40 minutes more survivors were ferried to shore by the *BURGERMEESTER VAN DAMME* and the *FIGHTER* while helicopters airlifted the more seriously injured. At 2240 reporters boarded requesting to view and to photograph bodies. They were ordered back into the tug and, at this time, complied with the order.

Up to 2250 the *COWDENBURG* had been co-ordinating the rescue on board the *HERALD*. Her C.O. then nominated Chief Officer Shakesby of the *DUKE OF ANGLIA* as on scene commander. He in turn nominated *DUKE OF ANGLIA* (Captain J. Scott) as co-ordinating vessel. At that time he was unaware of any shore centre and was in VHF communication with his own ship. This appears to have worked very well as language difficulties were eliminated.

About this time *EUROPEAN CLEARWAY* (ex Dover) anchored near the wreck and offered assistance. Persons with knowledge of the *HERALD* were requested by O.S.C. and these were subsequently supplied by *EUROPEAN CLEARWAY, EUROPEAN TRADER* and *FREE ENTERPRISE VI* which had also arrived from Dover and was searching the area.

Mr. Shakesby now appears to have gained overall control of the situation on board and was making continued requests for lights, ladders, stretchers and plans of the vessel. Most of these requests were met, except that lighting was never adequate and eventually diving had to cease due to the extreme danger within the darkened hull. The *ARCO AVON*, which arrived on scene and anchored earlier, supplied hand lamps, but these did not arrive until much later.

During the time from the capsize the surviving crew of the *HERALD* had been engaged in rescue work and had been the initiators of the breaking of windows and lowering of ropes and ladders to haul up passengers. They did remarkable work. In most cases they themselves had first been rescued. Suffering from cold and shock they were persuaded to embark in *BURGERMEESTER VAN DAMME* for food and drink, and it was thought advisable to evacuate them to shore. it must be said though, that many wished to stay aboard and continue the rescue.

By 2330 it was apparent that most of the survivors above water level had been rescued and divers were organised to begin recovering bodies while still searching for survivors.

At 2335 the tugs *FIGHTER* and *RIVER TAMAR*, the latter with reporters, who had refused the Master's request to leave the ship after jumping aboard in Zeebrugge, were back alongside. *FIGHTER* was requested to prepare her foredeck for bodies as no space remained on the *HERALD*.

Shortly after this reporters climbed aboard the *HERALD* and became an impediment to the operations. They refused to leave until the OSC threatened them with physical removal.

By 2350 the hand lamps were failing and more were requested. Most of the visible bodies had been recovered and the divers were withdrawn from the darker recesses of the hull.

At 0030 divers were despatched in an inflatable craft to hammer on the bottom of the wreck because there was no obvious access to the engine room. Officers and seamen from the other Townsend ships who were familar with the *HERALD* layout arrived and more hand lamps became available. Further searches were then carried out.

At 0115 three survivors were found in the forward drivers' accommodation. It must be assumed that these were the last to be found alive. Shortly after this plans of the vessel arrived. Sub-Lieutenant Cox *(H.M.S. HURWORTH)* organized a search with the U.K. and Belgian clearance diving teams. At 0145 diving was again suspended until more lights became available at 0215. Thereafter systematic searching of the vessel continued. Helicopter movements were suspended to make it possible to communicate and to listen for hammering.

The tide was now rising rapidly through the vessel. It was decided to suspend diving, after completion of the systematic search, until daylight and a fall in the water level.

At 0315 *DUKE OF ANGLIA* handed rescue co-ordination to *H.NL.M.S. MIDDLEBERG*. Shortly after a final search, which included the engine control room, the operation was completed.

The OSC requested permission to hand over to the salvage teams which had arrived. This was granted at 0325. All teams left the *HERALD* until daylight.

APPENDIX III

The following ships are reported to have taken part in the rescue operation:

SANDERUS	– Belgian dredger
RIVER TAMAR	– British – Whitbury Shipping Company
DUKE OF ANGLIA	– British
GABRIELE WEHR	– German
NORDIC FERRY	– British – Townsend Thoresen Car Ferry
EUROPEAN CLEARWAY	– British – Townsend Thoresen Car Ferry
EUROPEAN TRADER	– British – Townsend Thoresen Car Ferry
FREE ENTERPRISE VI	– British – Townsend Thoresen Car Ferry
FREE ENTERPRISE VIII	– British – Townsend Thoresen Car Ferry
ARCO AVON	– British dredger
BURGERMEESTER VAN DAMME	– Belgian tug
SEA HORSE	– Belgian tug
SEA LION	– Belgian tug
FIGHTER	– Belgian tug
ZEEBRUGGE 1	– Belgian crane barge
CROCUS	– Minesweeper – Belgian Navy
EKSTER	– Tug – Belgian Navy
VALCKE	– Tug – Belgian Navy
ZEEMEEUW	– Belgian Navy
KREKEL	– Belgian Navy
BIJ	– Belgian Navy
SPA	– Belgian Navy
MIDDLEBURG	– Dutch Minesweeper
HMS HURSWORTH	– British – Royal Navy
FGS GOETTINGEN	– German
CAPRICORN	– French Navy – Minesweeper
No. 1 MAIN LIFEBOAT	– Belgian Lifeboat Service
No. 4 INSHORE LIFEBOAT	– Belgian Lifeboat Service
No. 19 INSHORE LIFEBOAT	– Belgian Lifeboat Service
WATER POLICE	– Belgian
PILOT BOAT	– Belgian
NORMA	– Belgian Crane Barge

APPENDIX IV

Model and full scale experiments

BMT carried out investigations at the request of the Department in three main areas:–

1. Detailed computations of flooding, squat and track simulation.

2. Model experiments on squat, bow wave entry and sheering.

3. A full scale trial on the *PRIDE OF FREE ENTERPRISE* at Zeebrugge

As to 1:

Calculations were made as to the dynamic sinkage of the vessel, both bodily and in terms of trim, at a representative depth of 16.5 m and also at a reduced depth of water of 12.2 m. The calculations and the later model experiments were carried out at the ship draught of 5.69 m which was then regarded as the most probable mean draught of the vessel at the time of the casualty. It was later that the possibility appeared that the vessel was deeper by perhaps 0.2 m. The trim used was 0.28 m. The squat experiments and the calculations showed that at say 16 knots, the vessel would sink relative to the static sea surface by 0.58 m with a small change of trim by the head of 0.18 m. Thus the effect of trim would be small, if real, but the reduction of general freeboard produced by dynamic sinkage would be important.

Flooding calculations using the NMI FLOOD program were carried out for a mean draught of 5.54 m, a trim by the head of 0.49 m and a GM (fluid) of 1.70 m. This program allowed real time calculations of the displacement, stability and attitude of the vessel and of the water level in the vehicle deck as flooding through the door openings took place. Once substantial capsize angles had been reached the program could not continue because so many subsidiary assumptions would become necessary, such as the integrity of various parts of the superstructure and deckhouses, the stability and positioning of the vehicles on the vehicle decks, etc. However the flooding calculations indicated quite clearly that once water started to enter the vessel there would be an initial very rapid lurch to around 30°, this taking place in approximately 6–7 seconds. A steady heel of 25–30° lasted for a short time and then the capsize proceeded. Professor Steneroth's calculations, which were based on different considerations, namely the entry of water plus the centrifugal heeling moment effect of this water with the ship in a turn, also indicated this very rapid lurch and then a stop and then finally an increase in angle of heel but again at a much lower rate. This initial lurch to an angle of the order of 30° as shown by both the NMI FLOOD and Steneroth calculations is a valuable confirmation of the evidence of a number of passengers and crew who were convinced that the vessel started to list slowly and then suddenly lurched to about 30° throwing people from the starboard side of the ship to port with observed violence.

The Court is satisfied that the mechanism for this lurch was that the water entering the vehicle deck made the ship unstable causing a roll to port but that this water then lay in the lower side of the vehicle deck and the ship returned to temporary stability due to picking up righting lever and adopting a temporary angle of loll. Thereafter water continued to enter through the bow doors and the angle of loll increased progressively until eventually the ship was on her beam ends.

Further calculations were carried out by BMT to simulate the track of the vessel and while there were simplifications in this simulation computation – for example treating the vessel as a single screw ship – nevertheless the results were interesting and helpful. It was shown, for example, both by calculation and model experiment, that with a port heel there would be a strong coupling effect between port heel and yaw to starboard. This would account for much of the known yaw that actually occurred. The vessel came to rest on a heading very nearly reciprocal to that of her original course. The helmsman had warned the Master in the early stages of the final capsize that he could not control the vessel's turn to starboard even with full port helm. This was the first intimation that Captain Lewry had of anything untoward.

One effect that was not taken into account by BMT was that as the vessel's heel or list became large, the port screw would be deeply immersed, still thrusting effectively, while the starboard screw and the rudder would be emerging and becoming ineffective. Clearly this would increase the tendency for the vessel to turn to starboard.

The simulation computations concluded that the time of passing the outer breakwater was some 19 minutes after departure (18:24 as against 18:23/24 from evidence) with 3 to 6 minutes thereafter to the final grounding. (18:27 – 18:30 hours if 18:24 be taken as the time of passing the Outer Mole.)

BMT concluded that the start of the Capsize scenario would be 1.5 to 2.0 minutes after passing the Outer Mole and going to Combinator 6. The simulation computations also concluded that a time of well over 60 seconds was required between the start of the capsize and the final resting at past 90°. Professor Steneroth concluded less, perhaps about ½ minute, but in both cases a number of assumptions have had to be made which may not have been realistic. In particular, Professor Steneroth considered that the vessel must have been on a curved track to starboard from immediately after leaving the Mole to the time of start of capsize, perhaps half a minute before reaching the wreck position. This presupposed that this very considerable turn to starboard would not be noticed by the helmsman or by the Master, in spite of the helmsman steering by compass and having lights ahead of the vessel available for reference and the Master alternating between the conning position and the radar during this time. The Court cannot accept Professor Steneroth's interpretation because it is most unlikely that such a turn would not have been noticed, in particular by Captain Lewry. There is no reason to think that Captain Lewry's navigation was in any way at fault or that he was not keeping a good lookout.

The BMT calculations assume that the ship first reached a large angle of heel of the order of 90° only when she reached the wreck site. It was and is impossible to quantify the final sinking of the vessel. The temporary but quite considerable buoyancy of the deckhouses may have allowed the vessel to continue to move for some appreciable time while nearly upon her beam ends. We do not consider that a detailed explanation of this part of the sinking is material. What is clear from the BMT simulation is that there is a good explanation of the turn to starboard against the helm while the final turn onto the wreck heading may have been increased to some extent by pivoting about the deckhouses on the sea bed.

As to 2:

Extensive model testing was carried out on a model 3.397 m in length representing the *HERALD* up to and including the level of G deck. The model was self-propelled with three fixed pitch screws and an operating rudder at the stern. It had the bow rudder and the bow propeller modelled but not operable, the propeller being in the full feathered mode. Bilge keels were fitted. The bow opening to the lower vehicle deck was modelled complete with doors which could be left open or could be shut. To prevent the model sinking when flooding took place through the open bow doors a bulkhead was fitted across the vessel between the entry longitudinal bulkheads at Station 8.5, approximately at the position of the inner water tight door. The model was powered through umbilical wires which also gave engine control and was capable of full steering by radio control.

The tests were carried out in the Number 2 Basin at Feltham which has a 76 m long shallow water section modelled with a smooth dimensionally accurate hard bottom. The entry to this is from deeper water. The water in the shallow portion was kept at a scale 16.5 m depth. Both free running and captive tests were carried out. The model was run up to any desired speed in the deep water section arriving at this speed when entering the shallow portion. Video records were taken of the conditions at the bow door and an accurate speed was obtained for each run. Runs were made over a range of speeds and at several draughts and over a range of trims. In the captive tests a number of runs were made with a scale water depth of 12.2 m.

It was found that with many of these combinations there was a critical speed below which water did not enter the open bow door. Below the critical speed water was thrown forwards and sideways by the spade and the bow. As soon as the critical speed was reached a quite sharp transition took place and water began to flow aft into the vehicle deck. In the case of the model the water was stopped by the transverse bulkhead. This critical speed was sensitive to trim at any given mean draught. The effect for any particular freeboard forward was so well defined that critical speed against draught or trim could be plotted as a definite line. The critical speed was found to be sensitive to water depth, for instance reducing by about 2½ knots when in water 12.2 m deep compared with 16.6 m deep, both with a bow freeboard of 2.5 m.

Some tests were carried out with a 15° heel. These demonstrated coupling between yaw and heel. With no trim 10° of rudder was required to hold course. With 0.72 m trim by the head and 15° heel to port a sheer to starboard developed and green water was taken over the spade at a freeboard where little or no water entered with the model upright. The model tests showed that the ship had adequate power to maintain at least 18 knots in water of 16.5 m depth and that trim by the head did not give rise to any handling problems.

As to 3:

The final experimental work was a full scale trial of the *PRIDE* at Zeebrugge. Elaborate instrumentation was installed so that the vessel's position and heading at all times could be determined with accuracy. Two complete Racal-Decca Trisponder radio location systems were used with an accuracy of + 1 metre and additionally four theodolite shore based stations were set up. The vessel speed was measured by logs and by calculation from the known position at any time.

Three runs were made. The first was from the berth and more or less simulated the actual path and events aboard the *HERALD* on the night of the casualty. Mean water depth was 16.6 m. The second run was on a reciprocal course from a position at sea in 14.5 mean depth and the third, an outward bound course again, in the same depth as the first run.

For all the runs the intention was to load the vessel into what was then thought to be the casualty condition. In the event the trim by the head was less than at the time of the casualty being under 0.3 m whereas at the casualty it was probably over 0.6 m. The draught also was probably less than that at the actual casualty, namely 5.69 m mean as against 6.65 m (lower bound) and 5.82 m (upper bound). The effect of this would be that the critical speed for water to flow aft in quantity over the bow spade would be higher on the trial of the *PRIDE* than it would be for the *HERALD* on the night of the casualty. From the BMT model tests the upper bound casualty condition critical speed would appear to be about $16\frac{1}{4}$ knots and in the lower bound condition 17 knots.

A detailed condition was calculated by the Townsend Thoresen Consultants, Messrs. Three Quays, using the vessel's declared lightship from the Builder's inclining and the anticipated tank conditions for consumables. Vehicles were arranged that would give the required balance of weight to make up the casualty displacement. However it was found that a considerable amount of the cargo arranged could not be accepted and had to be shut out as the vessel was on the required draughts. These were read accurately by means of draught sticks and stilling tubes.

The vessel put to sea and within reasonable limits paralleled the course and actions of the *HERALD* on the night of the casualty. When Combinator 4 was set the speed increased from the speed at Combinator 2/3 of 10 knots to 14.1 knots, this increase taking 4 minutes. Upon setting Combinator 6, the speed increased from 14.1 knots to 18 knots in $2\frac{1}{2}$ minutes.

There was some evidence that *PRIDE* is inherently a slightly faster ship than was *HERALD* but any such difference would be small and probably only one or two decimal points of a knot. Also the casualty draught was almost certainly rather greater than the trial draught for the *PRIDE*. We consider, therefore, that the *HERALD* would reach a steady speed probably just under 14 knots on Combinator 4 and perhaps $17\frac{3}{4}$ knots on Combinator 6.

Video records were taken of the behaviour of the bow wave at various speeds during this trial. There was a slight head sea and hence on the voyage out (Run 1) there was some intermittency in the boarding of water over the bow spade. On Run 2 the vessel was heading down the waves and no such effect was observable, as might be expected. On Run 3 the heading was again into the seas but in shallower water.

Of particular interest were the records taken by a camera looking down from the forecastle head on the bow doors and the spade. From these records and the model tests it was clear that the quite sharply defined critical speed for water to flow over the spade and aft was 17.6 knots for the *PRIDE* at the trim and draught applying. The bow doors were, of course, shut but had they been open at 17.6 knots the vessel would have taken a dive similar to that taken by the *HERALD*. As described, for the *HERALD* on the night of the accident, it is probable that the critical speed was less due to the deeper draught and the greater trim and was probably about $16\frac{1}{4}$ knots.

BMT computed a simulation for the speeds of *HERALD* and the results from this and from the *PRIDE* trial show that water would start to enter through the bow door aperture at the following intervals after setting Combinator 6:

PRIDE	Trial	2.4 minutes
HERALD	Lower bound condition	1.6 minutes (based on trial)
	Upper bound condition	1.1 minutes (based on trial)
	Lower bound condition	1.3 minutes (based on simulation)
	Upper bound condition	0.7 minutes (based on simulation)

We are satisfied that water would start to flood through the bow door aperture probably just under one minute after Captain Lewry set the Combinators to Position 6. His evidence is that this was done at the Outer Mole.

We conclude that the likely time of events was as follows:–

Departure	18:05 GMT		
Passed inner breakwater	18:20		
Passed Outer Mole	18:23	or	18:24
(Simulation calculations passed Outer Mole)	18:24		
Combinator 6 set	18:23	or	18:24
Water over bow sill	18:24	or	18:25
Mr. Butler heard water on stairs	18:25		
Bridge Clock stopped	18:28		
Capt. Lewry opinion capsize 4 minutes after passing Outer Mole	18:27	or	18:28
(Simulation calculations completion capsize)	18:27	to	18:30

Questions and Answers

The Court's answers to the questions submitted by the Secretary of State for Transport are as follows:

Q.   1.   What caused the *HERALD OF FREE ENTERPRISE* to capsize on the 6th March 1987?

A.   The ship put to sea with her outer and inner bow doors fully open, and thereafter, as speed built up, water entered on to the vehicle deck in large quantities and destroyed her stability. The ship then capsized rapidly.

Q.   2. (a) Was a proper rescue operation conducted after the capsize of the *HERALD OF FREE ENTERPRISE*?

  (b) How many lives were lost following the capsize of the *HERALD OF FREE ENTERPRISE*?

A.   (a) Yes; see Report.

  (b) At least 188.

Q.   3.   Was the capsize of the *HERALD OF FREE ENTERPRISE* caused or contributed to by the fault of any person or persons and, if so, whom and in what respect?

A.   Yes.

  By the faults of the following:–

  1.   Mr. Mark Victor Stanley.

  2.   Mr. Leslie Sabel.

  3.   Captain David Lewry.

  4.   Townsend Car Ferries Limited at all levels from the Board of directors through the managers of the Marine Department down to the Junior Superintendents.

  As to the respects in which each of the above-named was guilty of causative fault, see Report.

71

Q. 4. (a) What lessons can be learnt from the circumstances of, and the practices relating to, the embarkation of passengers, the loading of freight and preparing the *HERALD OF FREE ENTERPRISE* for sea and the subsequent casualty?

   (b) What steps should be taken to avoid a similar capsize in the future?

   (c) What steps should be taken to minimise loss of life in the future if a similar capsize were to occur?

A. (a) There are lessons to be learned in all the areas referred to in the questions. (See Report)

   (b) Proper procedures for ensuring that the bow and stern doors are closed before proceeding to sea. (See Report)

   (c) See Report.

Q. 5. What steps should be taken to reduce the possibility of a Ro-Ro ferry capsizing if her watertight integrity is breached in other circumstances?

A. Consideration should be given to increasing the reserve buoyancy of a Ro-Ro vessel and to restricting the spread of water on the bulkhead deck.

Hon. Mr. Justice Sheen, *Wreck Commissioner*

Dr. E. Corlett, *Assessor*

Mr. C. A. Sinclair, *Assessor*

Commodore G. G. Greenfield, *Assessor*

Captain E. G. Venables, *Assessor*

SUPPLEMENTARY REPORT ON COSTS

The jurisdiction of a Wreck Commissioner to make an order for the payment of any part of the costs of a Formal Investigation is derived from subsection (5) of section 56 of the Merchant Shipping Act 1970, which provides that "The Wreck Commissioner may make such an order with regard to the costs of the investigation as he thinks just".

Rule 14 of the Merchant Shipping (Formal Investigations) Rules 1985 provides:–

> "Where the Wreck Commissioner orders the costs and expenses of the formal investigation or any part thereof to be paid by a party other than the Secretary of State, he shall state in a report his reasons for making such an Order."

The wording of that Rule suggests that it would be normal for the Secretary of State to pay the costs and expenses of the investigation. Other parties may incur such additional costs as they think fit.

After the Report of the Court had been read there were applications on behalf of all parties other than Townsend Car Ferries Limited that the whole or part of their costs should be paid either by the Secretary of State for Transport or by Townsend Car Ferries Limited. On behalf of the Secretary of State, Mr. Steel made an application that Townsend Car Ferries Limited pay the whole or a substantial part of the costs of the first part of this Inquiry. The second part of the Inquiry, which lasted 9 days, was concerned with the question: what steps should be taken to improve the safety of Ro/Ro ferries in the future? As that question is asked for the benefit of the travelling public, it is right that the costs of that part of the investigation should be borne by the public purse.

The circumstances which give rise to a Formal Investigation are so infinitely varied that I shall not attempt to lay down any general principles applicable to all Investigations. The statutory power of a Wreck Commissioner to make an order for costs is laid down in the most general terms. It is not for me to attempt to define that which Parliament has not defined. However in the commentary by Mr. A.R.G. McMillan upon Rule 16 of the 1923 Shipping Casualties etc. Rules, which is to be found on page 109 of Mr. McMillan's book entitled "Shipping Inquiries and Courts" published in 1929 there appears the following sentence:

> "Frequently, the order for costs is used as a method of penalising parties, and, as against parties other than certificated officers, is, with censure, the only form of penalty competent to the court."

That has always been accepted as a correct principle. It was well-known when the Merchant Shipping Act 1970 was enacted. If Parliament had then thought that an order for costs ought not to be used as a method of penalizing parties, it would have made that clear in section 56. In case this Order should be challenged in a higher court, I wish to make it clear that I have adopted that principle.

After hearing the submissions of all counsel who made applications for an order for costs in favour of their clients I have reached the conclusion that justice will be done in the circumstances of this case by the five orders which I have made. In making those orders and no other orders I have borne in mind that the costs which are not recovered by reason of those orders will lie where they have fallen except where there have already been agreements between the parties as to those costs. I am required by Rule 14 to state my reasons for making the third and fifth order. I will state my reasons for making each of the orders.

My reasons are as follows:

As to (1): Mr. Stanley was represented separately from the other members of the crew. It was necessary that he should be made a party to the Investigation and it was right that he should be separately represented. No unnecessary costs were incurred on his behalf. He was unable to obtain Legal aid, but it is just that the public purse should bear the cost of legal representation. This was not disputed.

As to (2): Townsend Car Ferries Limited undertook to pay the costs (on an indemnity basis) of legal representation of the dependants of the victims and of 155 survivors. But Mr. Steel, on behalf of the

Secretary of State, recognized that there are grounds for saying that the costs incurred in investigating matters of future safety should be borne by the public. Accordingly I have ordered the Secretary of State to make a contribution of £10,000 towards their costs.

As to (3): The participation of Steggles Palmer and their counsel on behalf of surviving members of the crew, the dependants of those members of the crew who died and the National Union of Seamen was welcomed by Counsel for the Secretary of State. No unnecessary costs were incurred on their behalf. They made a useful contribution to the Inquiry. It seems to me to be just that Townsend Car Ferries Limited should make a substantial contribution to the costs incurred by the National Union of Seamen. My reasons for saying that are these:–

(a) It is right that the dependants of all those who died and all who suffered injury or loss should be represented.

(b) Townsend Car Ferries Limited were partly to blame for the casualty and should bear the cost of this legal representation.

(c) It is unnecessary to make an order that the Secretary of State pays these costs and a further order that he recovers them from Townsend Car Ferries Limited. I have considered whether it is right to make an order that a party other than the Secretary of State should be ordered to pay the costs of any other party on the grounds that Townsend Car Ferries Limited were not asked whether they had any objection to Mr. Owen's clients being made a party to the Inquiry. But it seems to me that when there can be no doubt about the correctness of the decision as to who should be a party to the Investigation the Court has power to make such an order if it is just.

As to (4): Captain David Lewry and Mr. Leslie Sabel have both been found guilty of serious negligence causative of the casualty. Both these officers have suffered the penalty of having their Certificates suspended. The Court does not wish to impose on them a heavy financial penalty. Fortunately for them they have been represented at the expense of their Union. However part of the Investigation was devoted to matters which prolonged it more than would have been necessary to deal with their negligence alone. For this reason the Secretary of State should make a contribution towards their costs. I have assessed that contribution at £25,000.

As to (5): On behalf of Townsend Car Ferries Limited, Mr. Clarke made a number of points, of which the most important were the following:

(a) His instructing solicitors have made a great contribution to the Investigation and they and their clients have conducted themselves responsibly.

(b) At an early stage Townsend Car Ferries Limited admitted fault by letter and further, on the second and eighth days of the Inquiry, by their counsel make useful and realistic admissions.

(c) Many of the matters investigated in the first part of the Investigation were matters of public interest for future safety and not matters which were causative of the casualty.

(d) This Investigation was for the benefit of the public and the cost of it should be borne by the public.

Mr. Steel submitted that the mere fact of a finding of fault does not necessarily carry an order for costs with it. He invited me to consider in respect of each party the degree of culpability, the level at which faults lay and the causative significance of those faults. Mr. Steel further pointed out that admissions made in an Investigation are not to be equated with admissions in civil litigation. Despite the admissions made by Townsend Car Ferries Limited, the first part of this Investigation was still necessary because of the seriousness of the casualty, the large number of deaths and the need to make it clear that nothing was being hidden from the public.

For the reasons stated in the Report Townsend Car Ferries Limited have to bear a heavy responsibility for the disaster.

Although it may be said that there was no direct connection between this disaster and (a) the carrying of an excessive number of passengers and (b) the overloading of the ship, it is clear that the whole Investigation has stemmed from the disaster. All parts of it were relevant. Indeed there was no objection taken to any of the evidence on the grounds of relevance. No time was wasted.

There being no other way in which this Court can mark its feelings about the conduct of Townsend Car Ferries Limited other than by an order that they should pay a substantial part of the costs of this Investigation, I have ordered them to pay the sum of £350,000. That seems to me to meet the justice of the case.

Wreck Commissioner

Printed in the United Kingdom for Her Majesty's Stationery Office
Dd240184 3/88 C15 398 12521